VALIDATE YOUR OFFER

A 28-day profit blueprint to sell before you create and turn ideas into income as a writer, coach, or speaker

Jonathan Milligan

PGB

PLATFORM GROWTH BOOKS

YOUR FREE GIFT

As a way of saying thanks for your purchase, we are offering a free companion online course called, *The Validate Your Offer Accelerator Course.*

With this companion online course, you'll be able to fully implement all the exercises, worksheets, and checklists inside this book. To get free instant access, go to:

MarketYourMessage.com/validate-course

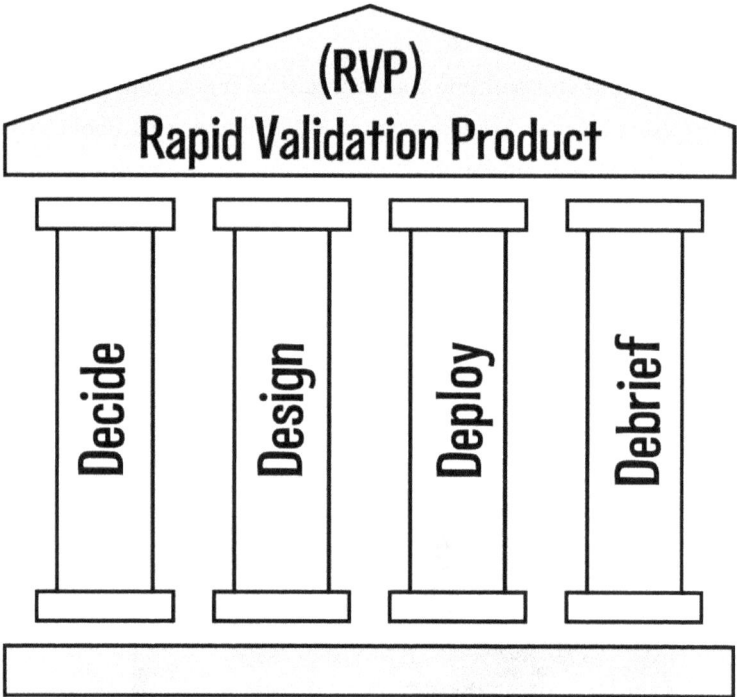

The Rapid Validation Product (RVP) Framework

Inside the pages of this book, you'll discover a powerful framework known as the RVP Method. To validate your offer, you need clarity on four things: Decide (your offer, topic, and deadline), Design (your rapid validation product), Deploy (your launch strategy), and Debrief (your improvement plan).

Contents

Introduction

Y ou launch, and then you learn.

It's hard to learn your way to results in life. Results only come from action. So, how do we get what we want without wasting a lot of time, energy, and resources?

I know firsthand how daunting it can be to put your idea out there. When I first started, I was plagued by doubts and fears. What if no one wants what I'm offering? What if I invest all this time and money only to watch my idea flop? The uncertainty was paralyzing.

But here's the thing: you don't have to risk it all to bring your vision to life.

Over the years, I've developed a proven system to quickly validate any business idea without wasting time, money, or resources. And in the pages of this book, I'll show you exactly how to do the same.

Imagine being able to test your idea with real paying customers in just a matter of weeks. Imagine gathering invaluable feedback and insights that help you refine your offer to perfection. Imagine launching with confidence, knowing that you've got a winner on your hands.

That's the power of rapid validation. And it's not just theory - I've used this exact process to validate and launch multiple successful products and services. I've seen it work time and time again, for myself and for countless others.

Now, I'm sharing my step-by-step validation blueprint with you. It's for writers, coaches, teachers, and speakers. This book will show you how to package your expertise into an offer people can't resist. You'll test it with your target audience and make your first sales - all in record time. No more guesswork. No more endless planning. No more fear of failure. Just a clear, proven path to turning your idea into income.

So, if you're ready to take action and make your business dreams a reality, you're in the right place. Let's dive in and start validating your offer today.

Your success story starts now.

1

The Rapid Validation Product (RVP) Framework

In the late 1930s, with the threat of war looming, the British Royal Air Force faced a daunting challenge. They needed a fighter plane that could outperform the German Luftwaffe, and they needed it fast. Enter the Supermarine Spitfire.

The Spitfire's journey from concept to combat-ready was a masterclass in rapid validation. The British didn't have the luxury of time. They couldn't afford to spend years perfecting every detail. Instead, they embraced a "fail fast, learn faster" mentality.

Reginald Mitchell led the design team. They started with a clear vision: a sleek, oval wing. It would give the Spitfire unmatched speed and maneuverability. But they didn't just rely on theory. They built prototypes quickly, testing and tweaking as they went.

Each iteration brought new insights. Wind tunnel tests revealed areas for aerodynamic improvement. Pilot feedback highlighted the need for better visibility. With every rapid cycle of design, build, and test, the Spitfire evolved.

The result? In just 12 months, the Spitfire went from a paper sketch to a force to be reckoned with in the skies over Britain. It proved instrumental in winning the Battle of Britain, turning the tide of the war.[1]

The Spitfire story is a powerful reminder of the importance of rapid validation. When you're starting a new idea, like a fighter plane or a business, you can't get stuck in endless planning and perfection.

Instead, take a page from the Spitfire playbook. Start with a clear vision, but be ready to test, learn, and adapt quickly. Embrace the power of prototyping. Seek out feedback from your target audience. And most importantly, don't be afraid to fail fast, because that's how you learn faster.

In this chapter, we'll dive deep into the art and science of rapid validation. You'll learn a powerful framework for testing your ideas quickly and efficiently so you can bring your vision to life with confidence. Get ready to strap in and take flight.

The Pitfalls of Creating Without Validating

You've got a groundbreaking idea for a new product or service. You're convinced it's going to change lives and disrupt industries. So, you pour your heart and soul into creating it. Late nights, gallons of coffee, countless hours of toil. Finally, after months (or even years) of hard work, you unveil your masterpiece to the world, waiting for the accolades to roll in.

But then...crickets. Tumbleweeds. Silence.

It turns out the market just doesn't want what you've built. Despite all your efforts, you've created something that nobody is willing to pay for. Ouch.

Sadly, this scenario is all too common. Entrepreneurs and creators often fall into the trap of building first and asking questions later. They assume that just because they think their idea is brilliant, everyone else will, too.

But here's the hard truth: your opinion doesn't matter nearly as much as the market's opinion. You must solve a real problem for your target audience. If not, they won't pay for it, no matter how clever it is.

The result? Wasted time, money, and effort. Not to mention the emotional toll of pouring your passion into something that falls flat.

But here's the good news: there's a better way.

The Power of Rapid Validation

What if you could test your idea quickly and cheaply before investing tons of resources into it? What if you could get real feedback from real potential customers and use that data to guide your creation process?

Enter the Rapid Validation Product (RVP) framework.

The RVP framework is all about creating a small, quick-to-launch version of your product or service. Think of it as a minimum viable product (MVP) on steroids. The goal isn't to create a perfect, polished final product. Instead, it's to create something just good enough to test the waters and see if there's real demand.

Launch a basic version of your idea. It will help you learn what your market really wants. You can see what features they love, what they could live without, and what problems they're really trying to solve.

With this data, you can then iterate and improve your offering. You can be confident that you're moving in a direction the market will support. You can avoid the pitfalls of creating in a vacuum and instead, create with the voice of the customer guiding your every move.

Best of all, you can do all of this quickly and with minimal investment. Instead of spending months or years building something that may or may not succeed, you can validate your idea in a matter of weeks.

So, if you're tired of wasting time and resources on ideas that flop, it's time to embrace the power of rapid validation. In the rest of this chapter, we'll dive into the nitty-gritty of how to apply the RVP framework to your own ventures. Get ready to fail fast, learn faster, and create products that the market truly craves.

The Four Pillars of Rapid Validation

Every time I want to test an idea, I follow four simple steps. When followed closely, these steps will help you save time, money, and resources. It will also help you to get feedback as quickly as possible. Remember, we launch, then we learn.

Pillar 1. Decide - Lay the Foundation

Every great structure starts with a solid foundation. In the RVP framework, that foundation is built on three key decisions:

1. Choose your validation product type. Will it be a low-content book, a mini-course, group coaching, or a virtual workshop? Each option caters to a different type of creator (writer, teacher, coach, or speaker), so pick the one that aligns with your strengths.

2. Select your topic. Don't try to be everything to everyone. Hone in on a specific problem that your target audience is itching to solve. The more focused you are, the easier it will be to create a compelling offer.

3. Set your timeline. The beauty of rapid validation is that it doesn't have to take forever. Challenge yourself to complete your validation offer in 28 days or less. This tight timeframe will keep you focused and prevent scope creep.

Think of these decisions like a blueprint for a house. An architect wouldn't start building without a clear plan. You shouldn't start your offer without a solid foundation. By making these three key decisions upfront, you set yourself up for success in the rest of the RVP process.

Pillar 2. Design - Create an Irresistible Offer

Now that you've got your foundation in place, it's time to design an offer that your target audience won't be able to resist. This is where the Offer Clarity Grid comes in.

The Offer Clarity Grid is a simple but powerful tool for crafting a compelling value proposition. It consists of four key questions:

1. Plot: What does the hero (your target audience) want?

2. Problem: What's stopping them from getting it?

3. Promise: What can you help them achieve?

4. Path: What are the 3-7 steps they need to take to get there?

By answering these questions, you can create an offer that speaks directly to your audience's desires and pain points. You'll be able to clearly communicate the value of your product and how it will solve their problems.

The importance of a clear value proposition can't be overstated. A 2018 study by the Nielsen Norman Group found that products with clear value propositions had a much higher conversion rate. The rate was 69% higher, on average. By using the Offer Clarity Grid, you can tap into this power and create an offer that practically sells itself.

Pillar 3. Deploy - Launch with a Bang

You've laid the foundation and designed an irresistible offer. Now, it's time to bring it to life with a strategic launch.

As marketing guru Seth Godin famously said, "If you build it, they will come only works in the movies. Social media is a 'build it, nurture it, engage them and they may come and stay' medium.[2]" In other words, launching your offer isn't a one-and-done affair. It requires thoughtful planning and execution.

To maximize your chances of success, focus on three critical elements:

1. Build anticipation. Start teasing your offer before it's even available. Give your audience a taste of what's to come and get them excited

2. Generate buzz. Leverage your existing networks and reach out to influencers in your space. Get people talking about your offer.

3. Create urgency. Use scarcity tactics like limited-time bonuses or a closing cart to encourage people to take action now.

As you deploy these tactics, keep in mind the four types of buyers: spontaneous buyers, methodical buyers, social buyers, and deadline buyers. Tailor your messaging and offers to appeal to each group.

By executing a well-planned launch, you'll be able to cut through the noise and get your validation offer in front of the right people at the right time. You'll also gather valuable data and feedback that you can use to refine your offer going forward.

Pillar 4. Debrief - Learn and Iterate

Congrats! You've launched your validation offer and gathered some initial results. But the RVP process doesn't stop there. The final pillar, Debrief, is where the real magic happens.

The Debrief phase aims to turn your validation experience into insights. You can use them to improve your offer and your business. To do this, you'll use two key tools: the Business Validation Decision Tree and the Debrief Strategy.

The Decision Tree helps you objectively assess if you should accept the offer as-is. It can also help you see if you should make tweaks or pivot in a new direction. It takes the emotion out of the equation and gives you a clear path forward based on the data.

The Debrief Strategy, on the other hand, is all about gathering qualitative feedback from your audience. What did they love about your offer? What could be improved? What questions do they still have? By actively seeking out this feedback, you can gain a deeper understanding of your market and how to serve them better.

The power of this iterative approach can be seen in the story of Zappos. When the online shoe retailer first launched, they offered a wide range of footwear. But based on customer feedback, they quickly pivoted to focus solely on shoes. This focus let them offer unmatched service and selection. That led to their sale to Amazon for a billion dollars.

By embracing the Debrief pillar, you too can turn your validation experience into a launchpad for success. You'll be able to continuously improve your offers, better serve your audience, and build a thriving business that stands the test of time.

Tying It All Together

The RVP framework is a powerful tool for bringing your ideas to life quickly and efficiently. Follow the four pillars: Decide, Design, Deploy, and Debrief. They let you validate your offers with confidence. You will know that you're creating something your audience truly wants and needs.

The journey of a thousand miles begins with a single step. The RVP framework is that first step, the launchpad that propels you toward your entrepreneurial dreams. So what are you waiting for? It's time to decide, design, deploy, and debrief your way to success.

Today's Exercise: The RVP Brainstorming Blitz

Are you ready to take the first step toward bringing your entrepreneurial dreams to life? Welcome to the RVP Brainstorming Blitz. It's a powerful exercise to help you generate many potential validation offer ideas using the RVP framework.

You have 30 minutes. In that time, you'll brainstorm many validation offer ideas. They will cover the four pillars of the RVP framework: Decide, Design, Deploy, and Debrief. By the end of this exercise, you'll have a list of exciting possibilities to explore and validate.

But before we dive in, let's address the elephant in the room. You might be thinking, "But I don't have any good ideas!" or "What if I can't come up with anything in 30 minutes?" Trust me, I've been there. The beauty of this exercise is that it's designed to silence your inner critic and unleash your creative potential.

So grab a piece of paper, a whiteboard, or your favorite digital note-taking tool. Divide your space into four quadrants, one for each pillar of the RVP framework. Set a timer for 30 minutes, and let's get started!

Step 1: Decide (5-10 minutes)

Begin in the Decide quadrant. Your goal is to brainstorm 5-10 potential validation offer topic ideas. These could be problems you've seen in your industry. They could be skills you're passionate about sharing. Or, they could be topics your audience has asked for help with. Don't worry about perfecting them - just get them out of your head and onto the page.

Step 2: Design (5-10 minutes)

Next, move to the Design quadrant. For each idea you generated in the Decide phase, jot down the specific problem it solves. Remember, the key to a compelling offer is a clear value proposition. By identifying the problem upfront, you'll be able to craft an offer that resonates with your target audience.

Step 3: Deploy (5-10 minutes)

Now, let's shift gears to the Deploy quadrant. For each idea, brainstorm 2-3 ways you could promote your validation offer. Here's the kicker: I want you to do this even if you have little to no existing audience. The goal is to start thinking creatively about how to get your offer in front of the right people.

Step 4: Debrief (5-10 minutes)

Finally, move to the Debrief quadrant. This is where the magic happens. For each validation offer idea, write down 2-3 survey questions you'd love to ask your target audience. These questions will help you gather valuable feedback and insights to refine your offer. For example, you might ask, "What's the biggest challenge you're facing with [problem]?" or "What would make this offer a no-brainer for you?"

When the timer goes off, take a step back and assess your ideas. Which ones feel the most exciting and feasible? Circle them, star them, or highlight them in your favorite color. These are the ideas you'll want to explore further.

Now, I know what you might be thinking. "This is great, but what do I do with all these ideas?" Don't worry, we'll dive into that throughout the rest of the book. The RVP Brainstorming Blitz is just the first step. It opens you to new possibilities and helps you find your best opportunities.

Remember, the key to success with the RVP framework is to take action. By doing this exercise, you've already taken a powerful step. You're moving towards validating your ideas and building a thriving business. So give yourself a pat on the back, take a deep breath, and get ready to dive into the rest of the RVP process.

Your entrepreneurial journey is just beginning, and the RVP Brainstorming Blitz is your launchpad. So buckle up, stay curious, and enjoy the ride. The world is waiting for your brilliant ideas!

Key Takeaways:

- The RVP framework provides a quick, low-risk way to test and validate your product idea before making a major investment

- The 4 pillars of Decide, Design, Deploy, and Debrief give you a step-by-step roadmap to execute your validation offer in 28 days or less

- Put the RVP framework into action. It will give you the insights to build products your audience desires. You'll also avoid the pitfalls of creating without validation.

2

Pillar 1. Decide (Your Three Key Decisions)

When Sal Khan started tutoring his cousin in math back in 2005, he had no grand plans to build an online education empire. He just wanted to help his family member learn. So he recorded some short video lessons and threw them up on a little-known site called YouTube.

Then something unexpected happened. Total strangers started watching Sal's videos. And they loved them! The comments gushed about how clear and helpful the lessons were.

Sal was blown away. He realized he might be onto something much bigger than family tutoring sessions. So he kept making more videos. And more. And more.

Before long, he took a leap of faith and quit his cushy hedge fund job to go all-in on his online teaching idea. Fast forward to today, and Khan Academy reaches millions of grateful students worldwide.

But here's the crazy part: Sal didn't spend months building out a fancy academy first. He started by validating his concept through a few simple YouTube videos. Those early comments proved there was real demand for what he wanted to teach.

Only then did Sal pour serious time and effort into fleshing out his vision. He proved the market first, then built to meet it. And that made all the difference.[3]

Sal's story perfectly captures what you'll learn in this chapter: the key to turning your ideas into income isn't to go big right out the gate. It's to choose a focused offer type and topic, validate it quickly, and let the market guide your next steps.

Get this right and you can save yourself months of wasted effort building offers no one wants. You can gain confidence to go all-in on winners. And you can grow your business with far less risk and guesswork.

So let's dive into the three crucial decisions that make speedy validation possible, shall we? Your offer type, your topic, and your timeline. Nail those and you'll be well on your way to Khan Academy-level success (minus the hedge fund detour).

The Painful Path Most People Take

Pop quiz: what's the usual course of action when a lightbulb idea strikes? Most people do this. They start dreaming up the best, biggest version of their product. You dive headfirst into creation mode, toiling away for weeks or months to bring your grand vision to life.

Finally, after pouring your blood, sweat, and tears into this labor of love, you unveil it to the world, awaiting the inevitable avalanche of sales.

Crickets.

Turns out, there isn't much of a market for your masterpiece after all. Despite all your hard work, you're left with a giant pile of content and a giant hole in your wallet to match. Womp womp.

Why Most Makers Crash and Burn

Where did we go wrong? The fatal flaw is creating a full-blown product without first validating that people actually want it. We assume our idea is brilliant, and everyone will happily throw money at it. But assumptions are dangerous things in business.

Building a complete offer with no proof of demand is like playing Russian roulette with your time and money. If your guess is off, all that effort goes down the drain. Even if the idea has potential, you've wasted precious resources creating more than the market calls for.

Worst of all, it's soul-crushing to see your magnum opus collect virtual dust. After such a lackluster launch, most people throw in the towel, convinced they're just not cut out for this.

The Savvier Shortcut to Success

But there's a better way. Before you get swept away in the excitement of a new idea, pause and make three critical decisions: your offer type, your topic, and your timeline.

By strategically choosing a focused, minimum viable version of your offer, you can validate demand much faster - in as little as a week or two. This speedy feedback loop lets you test the waters without sinking the ship.

If your scaled-down offer gets a positive response, you'll have the confidence (and cash) to build it out further. And if it falls flat, you can scratch it and move on to the next idea without losing your shirt.

The key is to sell before you build and let the market be your guide. Work smarter, not harder, right?

So, let's break down how to pick the optimal offer type, topic, and timeline for fast and fruitful validation. Your bank balance will thank you.

Your 3 Key Decisions (Type, Topic, Timeline)

In order to successfully complete pillar one, you need to make three primary decisions. We will cover each of these in more depth in the next chapter, but let's briefly take a look at each one.

Decision 1. Pick Your Validation Offer Type

First, you've got to decide what minimum viable product will be your vehicle for validation. There are four core options, each perfectly suited for different natural talents.

If writing is your jam, a low-content book (think workbook, journal, or planner) could be your golden ticket. Have a knack for breaking down complex topics into bite-sized lessons? A mini-course might be your best bet. Love helping people work through challenges in real time? Consider a group coaching boot camp. Or, if you're a gifted speaker, a live workshop could be your winning play.

Think about it like this: You wouldn't put diesel in a gasoline car and expect peak performance, right? The same goes for your offer. To create a truly magnetic MVP, you need a format that runs on your unique brand of fuel.

So take a beat to reflect on what medium allows you to shine brightest. By playing to your strengths, you'll be able to whip up a high-quality validation offer in record time. And that's what we're all about.

Decision 2. Select Your Validation Offer Topic

Now that you've got your offer type locked in, it's time to choose a specific, in-demand topic for your MVP. The secret sauce? Steering clear of broad, beginner-to-advanced concepts in favor of laser-focused ideas.

Four proven frameworks reveal these magnetic topics. They tackle the first problem beginners face, solve a common challenge, promise a quick win, or focus on a crucial subtopic of a larger subject.

This ain't just theory, either. An in-depth study of 100 top-selling courses found that the narrow, outcome-oriented ones outsold the expansive, start-to-finish options by a whopping three to one.

The takeaway is clear: Specificity sells. By niching down and drilling into one pressing pain point, you can create an irresistible offer that practically sells itself. Plus, a tightly defined topic is far easier to whip into a MVP than an epic, catch-all opus.

Decision 3. Choose Your Validation Offer Deadline

Last but not least, you need to put a firm expiration date on this validation mission. And trust me, you want to keep it snappy. Thirty days or less is the name of the game.

Why the rush? Because free time is the enemy of shipping. Given an open-ended runway, most of us will tinker and tweak until the end of time, trying to reach that mythical state of perfection.

However, as bestselling author Jon Acuff knows, constraints can be a creator's best friend. He wrote his Wall Street Journal bestseller in a mere 30 days, proving that a tight timeframe is a powerful antidote to inaction.

And remember, your goal right now isn't to craft a flawless master-piece - it's to get a minimum viable product out into the world at lightning speed. Perfection is a fairy tale, but progress is very much within reach.

By setting a hard 28-day cap on your validation venture, you'll force yourself to strip your offer down to its most essential, impactful core. No time for bells and whistles, just pure, concentrated value.

So light a fire under yourself and commit to going from zero to sold in under a month. Your future self will thank you when those first sales notifications start rolling in.

Today's Exercise: A Reflection Exercise

Alright, it's time for a little tough love and self-reflection. I want you to think back to the last time you had a brilliant idea for a product or offer that never quite made it across the finish line. We've all been there, so don't be shy.

Got it in mind? Great. Now, let's put that stalled-out project under the microscope and diagnose where things went off the rails. Grab a pen and paper (or your favorite digital note-taker) and jot down your answers to the following questions:

1. Type Trouble: Did you choose a clear, specific format for your offer, or did you try to be everything to everyone? Were you forcing yourself to create in a medium that didn't align with your strengths, like writing a book, when you're really a born speaker?

2. Topic Tangle: Was your topic broad, vague, or just plain boring? Did you try to cover too much ground, or did you zero in on a juicy, urgent pain point your audience was

desperate to solve?

3. Timeline Trap: Did you give yourself a firm deadline to complete your offer, or did you leave things open-ended? Were you allowing yourself to endlessly tinker and perfect, or did you set a hard stop to force yourself to ship?

Chances are, one (or all) of these three elements was missing or muddled. Maybe you tried to create an epic, all-encompassing course instead of starting with a quick win mini-offer. Perhaps your topic was too generic to truly resonate with your target market. Or it could be that without a clear due date, you let perfection paralysis take the wheel.

This exercise is not about beating yourself up. It's about getting valuable lessons so you can do better next time. By identifying where you went astray, you can course-correct and set yourself up for validation victory.

So take a good, honest look at your past misfires and write down your key takeaways. What will you do differently this time around? How will you ensure you choose the right offer type, nail down a crave-worthy topic, and stick to a strict timeline?

Write out your action plan for each of the three decisions. Then, commit to putting these insights into practice as you embark on your next validation adventure. With this newfound clarity and resolve, you'll be unstoppable.

Remember, every "failure" is just a stepping stone to success if you take the time to learn from it. So pat yourself on the back for having the courage to reflect and improve. Your next offer will thank you for it.

Key Takeaways:

- Testing your offer with a focused minimum viable product is faster, easier, and smarter. It's better than jumping straight to building a full product.

- Align your validation offer to your natural strengths as a writer, teacher, coach, or speaker to leverage your gifts

- Choose an urgent, specific topic and set a firm 28-day or less timeline to create and launch quickly, avoiding the temptation to overbuild

3

The 4 Validation Offer Types

The year is 1860, and the Pony Express has just taken the U.S. by storm. Teams of riders on horseback are delivering mail from Missouri to California in a mere 10 days—a speed unheard of at the time. People are blown away. They can hardly believe it's possible to get messages across the country so quickly.

But here's the thing. The Pony Express isn't just a cool new mail service. It's a validation offer. A test to see if people actually want faster communication. And boy, do they ever! The demand is through the roof.

The U.S. government takes notice. They see the writing on the wall. Faster communication is the future, and the Pony Express has just proven it. So, they start investing in a brand-new technology: the telegraph.

The telegraph is a game-changer. It can send messages across the country in a matter of minutes, not days. But building a nationwide telegraph network is a massive undertaking. It requires a ton of infrastructure and investment.[4]

Without the Pony Express, the government might have hesitated. They might have wondered, "Is this really worth it? Do people actually want this?" But thanks to the Pony Express, they knew the answer was a resounding "Yes!"

The Pony Express was a validation offer. It was a small-scale test that proved there was a hungry market for faster communication. And it paved the way for one of the most transformative technologies in history.

That's the power of a validation offer. It's a way to test your idea before you go all in. It's a way to make sure you're not wasting your time and resources on something nobody wants.

And that's what this book is all about. We're going to dive into four specific validation offers that you can use to test your own business ideas. Whether you're a writer, a coach, a teacher, or a speaker, there's a validation offer that's perfect for you.

So, buckle up and get ready to learn. By the end of this chapter, you'll have the tools you need to validate your own offer and turn your ideas into income. Just like the Pony Express did for the telegraph.

Why Validation Offers Matter

You've got a brilliant idea for a new product. Maybe it's a book, a course, a coaching program, or a signature talk. You're absolutely convinced it's going to be a hit.

So, you dive in headfirst. You spend months pouring your heart and soul into creating this thing. You write, you record, you design. You invest a ton of time and money into making it perfect.

Finally, it's ready. You launch it to the world, expecting a flood of sales and rave reviews. But instead, you hear crickets. Tumbleweeds. Your product falls flat, and you're left wondering what went wrong.

Sound familiar? It's a trap that so many creators fall into. They assume that just because they love their idea, everyone else will, too. They skip the crucial step of validating their offer and end up wasting a ton of resources on something that the market just doesn't want.

Here's the hard truth. Creating a product without validation is like playing Russian roulette with your time and money. Sure, you might get lucky and create a hit. But more likely, you'll end up with a dud that nobody wants to buy.

Why? Because you're not a mind reader. You can't just guess what your audience wants. And even if you think you know, you might be way off base. That's why validation is so important. It's like a crystal ball that shows you exactly what your market desires.

So, what's the solution? Simple. Instead of going all-in on a big, comprehensive product right away, start small. Create a fast, lean validation offer that you can test quickly and easily.

This could be a low-content book, a mini-course, a short coaching boot camp, or a paid workshop. Something that you can create in a matter of days or weeks, not months. Something that lets you dip your toe in the water and see if there are any bites.

The beauty of a validation offer is that it gives you real-world feedback and data. You'll see firsthand whether people are actually willing to pull out their wallets and pay for what you're offering. You'll get comments, questions, and reviews that show you what's working and what's not.

Armed with that information, you can refine your idea and create a product that you know your audience wants. You can avoid the heartache and frustration of pouring your soul into something that falls flat. And you can use your time and resources wisely, focusing on the things that actually move the needle.

In short, validation offers are like a secret weapon for creators. They're the key to unlocking your audience's desires and creating products that sell like hotcakes. So, if you're not using them, you're leaving money on the table.

The 4 Validation Offers

Alright, let's dive into the four validation offers that can help you test your ideas and get real-world feedback fast.

Validation Offer #1. Low-Content Book (Writers)

First up, we've got the Low-Content Book. This is perfect for all you writers out there. Instead of jumping straight into a full-length book, why not test the waters with a simpler workbook, journal, or planner? It's a great way to validate your book idea and get a feel for the publishing process without committing to a massive project.

Take Ryan Holiday, for example. He validated his book ideas by starting with blog posts. He then refined them into articles and short books before finally expanding to full-length works. By starting small and testing the market, he was able to create best-sellers that he knew his audience wanted.

Validation Offer #2. Mini-Course (Teachers)

Next, we've got the Mini Course. Calling all teachers! Before you pour your heart and soul into a comprehensive flagship course, why not create a mini version that focuses on a specific subtopic? It's a fantastic way to validate your course idea and get valuable feedback from your students.

Did you know that the average time to create an online course is 90-240 hours? That's a huge investment! But with a mini course, you can test the waters in a fraction of that time, lowering your risk and ensuring that your full course will be a hit.

Validation Offer #3. 4-Week Bootcamp (Coaches)

Moving on to the 4 Week Bootcamp. This one's for you, coaches! Running a short group coaching program is a great way to help your clients achieve a specific outcome. It also validates your coaching process. You can create content week-by-week based on your clients' needs and get real-time feedback on what's working and what's not.

Think of it like being a personal trainer. The bootcamp model lets you test your "workout plan" and adapt it to your clients' needs before offering longer engagements. It's an agile way to refine your methodology and make sure you're delivering real results.

Validation Offer #4. 1-Day Virtual Workshop (Speakers)

Finally, we've got the 1 Day Paid Workshop. Listen up, speakers! Running a short online workshop is a fantastic way to validate demand for your topic and refine your talk for higher-ticket speaking gigs. By teaching your target market how to solve a specific problem, you'll get valuable feedback on your content and delivery.

The best part? Paid workshops let you reach a wider audience. They also let you validate market demand. This is before pitching conference organizers or corporate clients. It's a low-risk way to test your ideas and make sure you're delivering content that people actually want to pay for.

So there you have it! Four powerful validation offers that can help you test your ideas and create products that your audience will love. Whether you're a writer, teacher, coach, or speaker, there's a validation offer that's perfect for you. So what are you waiting for? Get out there and start validating!

Today's Exercise: Choose Your Validation Offer

Alright, it's time to take action! Let's put everything we've learned into practice with a simple exercise that'll help you validate your idea and get the ball rolling.

First things first, take a good, hard look at your current idea. Which of the four validation offer types fits it best? Is it a low-content book, a mini course, a 4-week bootcamp, or a 1-day paid workshop? Don't overthink it - just go with your gut.

Got it? Great! Now, let's outline that validation offer. What specific problem does it solve for your target market? Maybe it's helping busy moms meal prep like a pro or teaching aspiring entrepreneurs how to create a killer business plan. Whatever it is, make sure it's something your audience is itching to learn.

Next, jot down 2-3 key elements you'll include in your validation offer. This could be a set of templates, a step-by-step guide, or a live Q&A session. The goal is to make it as valuable and irresistible as possible.

Now for the scary part - setting a deadline. I know, I know, deadlines can be intimidating. But trust me, they're the key to making things happen. So grab your calendar and pick a date within the next 14 days to create and launch your validation offer.

But don't just pick a date and forget about it! Schedule some time blocks in your calendar specifically to work on your validation offer. Whether it's an hour a day or a few solid chunks of time, make sure you're carving out dedicated space to get it done.

And here's the kicker - tell someone about your deadline. A friend, a family member, a colleague - anyone who'll hold you accountable. There's nothing like a little external pressure to light a fire under your butt and make sure you follow through.

So there you have it - a simple exercise to help you take the first step towards validating your idea. It might feel a little daunting at first, but trust me, once you get started, you'll be amazed at how quickly things start to come together.

And who knows - maybe 14 days from now, you'll be launching a validation offer that changes the game for your business. Wouldn't that be something?

So what are you waiting for? Get outlining, get scheduling, and get ready to validate your way to success!

Key Takeaways:

- Validating your offer through a small initial product lowers risk and provides real market feedback.

- The 4 core validation offers are low-content books, mini courses, group coaching bootcamps, and paid workshops. Choose the best fit for your idea.

- Launch your first validation offer quickly to start gathering data. Use what you learn to guide your core offer development.

4

The 4 Secrets to Finding Your Killer Topic Idea

A dad takes his two young daughters to the local amusement park on a sunny Saturday afternoon. He watches them ride the merry-go-round and eat cotton candy. He notices the old rides, the trash on the grounds, and the bored parents on benches. In that moment, an idea starts to take shape in his mind. What if there was a place where the whole family could have fun together? A clean, safe, immersive environment that sparked the imagination? That dad was Walt Disney, and the idea became Disneyland - and later, Disney World.[5]

See, Walt didn't just have a random idea. He noticed a problem - the amusement parks of the day weren't appealing to parents and kids alike. They were seedy, dirty, and frankly, kind of boring for adults. But he also spotted an opportunity. By creating a theme park that catered to the whole family, Walt knew he could fill a huge gap in the market. So, he took that first inkling of an idea and ran with it. And we all know how that turned out.

Now, you might be thinking, "That's great for Walt Disney, but what does that have to do with me?" Well, everything, actually. Because the secret to finding your killer book idea? It's not so different from Walt's approach. You've got to identify a problem your target audience is facing and then find a way to solve it with your unique skills and expertise.

Maybe you're a productivity coach. You've noticed that most time management advice ignores single parents. So you decide to create a mini course specifically for moms and dads trying to juggle work, kids, and everything in between. Or maybe you're a health coach who sees your clients struggling to stick to a workout routine. So, you create a 30-day fitness challenge with short, doable workouts and daily accountability check-ins.

The point is that your killer topic idea is out there - you just need to know how to look for it. And that's exactly what we're going to cover in this chapter. We'll cover four proven methods for coming up with ideas. They will make your ideal readers buy faster than you can say "bestseller." So grab a notepad, and let's get started.

Breaking Through the Idea Block: Strategies to Spark Innovation

You've got your notebook ready, your pen poised, and... nothing. Crickets. You rack your brain for the perfect topic idea, but everything feels either overdone or overwhelming. Sound familiar? Don't worry, you're not alone. Coming up with validation offer ideas is a struggle for most people. And it's not hard to see why.

For starters, there's the shiny object syndrome. You know, when you're scrolling through social media and see an ad for the latest "foolproof" business idea. Suddenly, your mind is racing with visions of passive income and beachside margaritas. So you jump on the bandwagon, only to realize that everyone and their grandma is doing the same thing. Cue the sad trombone.

Then there's the copycat approach. You see a competitor killing it with their coaching program or e-book, so you figure, hey, if it worked for them, it'll work for me, right? Wrong. Because here's the thing: just because an idea is successful for someone else doesn't mean it's the right fit for you or your audience. Plus, nobody wants a carbon copy. They want the real, authentic you.

And don't even get me started on analysis paralysis. You know that feeling when you've got so many ideas bouncing around in your head that you can't seem to land on just one? So you spend hours, days, even weeks weighing the pros and cons of each one until you're so overwhelmed that you just throw in the towel altogether.

But here's the harsh truth: none of these approaches work. Chasing shiny objects is like playing business whack-a-mole. Copying your competitors is a recipe for blending in instead of standing out. And getting stuck in your own head is a surefire way to stay stuck, period.

So what's the solution? It all comes down to one word: empathy. See, the key to coming up with killer validation offer ideas is to put yourself in your target audience's shoes. To really understand their needs, their challenges, their secret desires. Because when you do that, you'll start to see patterns emerge.

Maybe you'll notice that your audience is always complaining about the same pain point, like feeling too busy to cook healthy meals. Or maybe you'll spot a common goal they're all striving for, like launching a successful side hustle. Whatever it is, when you take the time to truly listen to your people, the ideas will start to flow.

But it's not enough to just understand your audience. You've also got to know how to tap into that knowledge in a strategic way. And that's where the four methods we're about to dive into come in. These are the same techniques that the most successful entrepreneurs use to come up with ideas that practically sell themselves.

So get ready to take some notes because we're about to unlock the secrets to finding your killer topic idea. And trust me, once you've got that in your back pocket, there'll be no stopping you.

The 4 Ways to Create a Killer Topic Idea

Alright, let's dive into the nitty-gritty. Here are four ways to come up with offer ideas that will have your target audience pulling out their credit cards.

Topic Idea 1. The First Problem Method

First up, we've got the "First Problem Method." This one's all about focusing on the very first challenge your audience faces when they're just starting out in your niche. Think about it - when you're a beginner, everything feels overwhelming. You don't know where to start, what to do first, or how to avoid common mistakes. That's where you come in. By creating an offer that solves that first problem, you'll be the hero they've been waiting for.

Imagine you're a doctor, and a patient comes to you with a nasty cough. You don't just throw a bunch of random medications at them and hope for the best, right? Nope, you start by identifying the root cause of that cough - is it a cold? Allergies? Something more serious? Once you've pinpointed the problem, you can prescribe the right treatment. The same goes for your audience. By identifying their "first problem," you can create an offer that nips it in the bud.

For example, let's say you're a blogging coach. You know that one of the biggest hurdles new bloggers face is choosing a niche. They're paralyzed by indecision, afraid of picking the wrong topic and wasting their time. Sound familiar? So why not create a mini course called "Discover Your Blog Niche"? You could help them find their passion, study their market, and narrow their options. Boom - first problem, solved.

Topic Idea 2. The Common Challenge Method

Next up, we've got the "Common Challenge Method." This is about identifying a challenge. Almost everyone in your audience struggles with it, no matter how experienced they are. And let's be real - for most people, that challenge is time management. We're all busy, we've all got a million things on our plate, and we're all trying to figure out how to squeeze more hours out of the day.

Don't believe me? Just look at the stats. The American Psychological Association found that over 80% of Americans feel stressed at work, and lack of time is one of the top reasons why. So, if you can create an offer that helps people be more productive and manage their time better, you've got a winner on your hands.

For example, you could create a low-content book called "The Ultimate Blogger's Productivity Guide." Fill it with your best tips and tricks for maximizing your time, staying focused, and getting more done in less time. Whether your reader is a newbie blogger or a seasoned pro, they'll appreciate the help.

Topic Idea 3. The Quick Win Method

But what if your audience is looking for something they can accomplish quickly? That's where the "Quick Win Method" comes in. The idea here is to pinpoint a specific goal or result that your audience can achieve fast - like, really fast. We're talking hours or days, not weeks or months.

Think about those old-school door-to-door vacuum salesmen. They didn't just show up on your doorstep and start talking about the features of their fancy new machine. No, they offered to give you a quick demonstration right then and there. They'd sprinkle some dirt on your carpet, fire up the vacuum, and boom - clean the floor in seconds. That quick win was enough to convince plenty of folks to pull out their wallets.

You can use the same principle in your offer. For example, you could put together a one-day virtual workshop called "How to Create and Sell Your Online Course in a Weekend." Focus on the key steps they need to take to get their course up and running fast without getting bogged down in all the details. The promise of a quick win will be hard to resist.

Topic Idea 4. The Splinter Method

Finally, we've got the "Splinter Method." This is about taking a piece of your larger body of work. It could be a coaching program, a course, or a methodology. You break off a smaller chunk to sell on its own.

As Dave Ramsey says, "You don't need to know everything to get started. Just focus on one small problem and be part of the solution." So take a look at your signature system or framework and see if there's one specific element you could splinter off and go deep on.

For example, let's say you teach a comprehensive system for attracting high-paying coaching clients. One key piece of that system is creating a lead magnet that really speaks to your ideal client's needs. So why not create a mini course called "Craft Your Client-Attracting Lead Magnet"? You could dive deep into lead magnets' psychology. You could share your top converting examples and walk them through creating their own. It's a small piece of your larger system, but it's an important one that your audience will be eager to learn.

Today's Exercise: Find Your Killer Topic Idea

Alrighty, it's time to put all this theory into practice. Grab a notebook, a whiteboard, or even the back of a napkin - whatever works for you. Set a timer for 15 minutes, and get ready to brainstorm like a boss.

Here's your mission, should you choose to accept it: come up with at least three validation offer ideas for each of the four methods we just covered. That is three ideas for the First Problem Method. And three for the Common Challenge Method. Also, three for the Quick Win Method and three for the Splinter Method. Aim for a total of 12 ideas minimum.

Now, I know what you might be thinking. "But what if my ideas are stupid? What if they've been done before? What if I can't come up with anything good?" Don't worry about that right now. Focus on rapid implementation. This is the time to let your creativity run wild and see what you come up with.

Remember, the goal here isn't to come up with the perfect idea right out of the gate. The goal is to generate as many potential ideas as possible so you've got a solid list to choose from when it's time to validate. So don't judge your ideas as they come to you - just write them down and keep going.

And hey, if you get stuck, don't be afraid to ask for help. Bounce ideas off a friend or colleague, or even hit up ChatGPT for some inspiration. The key is to keep that pen moving and those ideas flowing.

Trust me, by the end of this 15-minute brainstorming session, you'll have a treasure trove of potential topics to choose from. And who knows - one of them might just be the key to unlocking a whole new level of success for you and your business.

Key Takeaways:

• Empathy is key. Understand your audience's needs and create offers that solve their problems.

• Four proven methods: solve the first problem, address a common challenge, provide a quick win, or splinter your methodology.

• Brainstorm without judgment. Generate as many ideas as possible to find the best ones.

• Take action. Pick an idea and run with it, refining it as you go.

• Your killer validation offer is out there. Trust the process and stay focused on your audience.

5

Selecting Your Rapid Validation Timeline

A British naval historian named Cyril Northcote Parkinson is scratching his head. It's the 1950s, and he's noticed something peculiar about the bureaucracies he's studied. As they grow, they seem to get less and less efficient. More people, more paperwork, more meetings, but less getting done. It's like the work is expanding to fill the time available, no matter how much time that is.

Parkinson turns this observation into a humorous adage: "Work expands so as to fill the time available for its completion.[6]" It's a clever way of saying that if you give someone a week to do a task, they'll find a way to make it take a week. Give them a month, and they'll make it take a month. The work grows to fit the time, like a goldfish in a bowl.

But here's the thing: Parkinson's Law isn't just a funny observation. It's a powerful insight that holds a crucial lesson for anyone trying to validate a new offer or idea. When you're launching something new, it's tempting to give yourself all the time in the world. After all, more time means you can make it perfect, right?

Wrong. As Parkinson observed, more time just means more procrastination. It means more second-guessing and more busy work. The key to rapid validation is to do the opposite: embrace short timelines that force you to focus on what really matters.

In this chapter, we'll dive into the power of tight deadlines and explore how you can use them to your advantage when validating your offer. Shorter timelines are often better than longer ones. I'll give you some specific options for making your own Rapid Validation Prototype (RVP) schedule. By the end, you'll have a clear plan for testing your idea quickly and efficiently without falling prey to Parkinson's Law.

So, get ready to think differently about timelines. It's time to ditch the idea that more time equals better results and embrace the power of positive constraints. As Parkinson might say, "If you want something done, give it to a busy person." Let's get busy validating your offer!

Selecting the Right Timeframe for Rapid Implementation

Let's talk about the elephant in the room: most people struggle with setting project timelines. When we're launching something new, whether it's a book, a course, or a coaching program, our first instinct is often to give ourselves a ton of time. We think, "This is a big, important project. I need to make sure I have enough runway to do it right."

Sound familiar? Here's the problem with that approach: it's a recipe for procrastination and paralysis. When we give ourselves too much time, we tend to fill that time with busy work and second-guessing. We endlessly tinker with the details. We think that if we keep tweaking, we'll make something perfect.

But perfection is a myth. And while we're chasing it, momentum dies. Weeks turn into months, and before we know it, we've lost steam, and our once-exciting project has become a dreaded albatross.

So what's the alternative? Embrace the power of short, focused timelines. When we give ourselves less time to validate an offer, magic happens. Suddenly, we're forced to prioritize ruthlessly. We don't have time for busy work or perfectionism. We have to focus on what really matters: creating something valuable and getting it in front of people.

Condensed timelines create a sense of positive pressure. They light a fire under us and force us to make decisions quickly. And here's the counterintuitive thing: that pressure often leads to better results, not worse ones. When we have to move fast, we don't have time to overthink or second-guess. We have to trust our instincts and take decisive action.

But the benefits of short timelines go beyond just speed. They also help us combat two of the biggest enemies of rapid validation: perfectionism and analysis paralysis. When we have a tight deadline, we can't afford to get bogged down in endless planning and theorizing. We have to put something out there and see how people respond.

And that's the key to rapid validation: getting real-world feedback as quickly as possible. You can spend months crafting the perfect offer in your head, but until you put it in front of actual people, you're just guessing. Shorter timelines force you to test your ideas in the real world, where it matters.

So if you want to validate your offer quickly and efficiently, embrace the power of short timelines. Don't fall into the trap of thinking that more time equals better results. Instead, focus on what really matters and use the power of positive constraints to drive momentum and real-world learning.

The 3 Rapid Validation Timelines That Work

Alright, so you're sold on the power of short timelines. But how do you actually choose the right timeline for your Rapid Validation Prototype (RVP)? Let's dive in and look at three options.

Option 1. The Weekend Warrior (14 days)

This is the fastest, most intensive timeline. You'll build your RVP in just 2-3 days, alongside 14 days of promotion. It's a full immersion, pedal-to-the-metal approach. If you thrive under pressure and want to validate your idea as quickly as possible, this might be the path for you.

Option 2. The Weekly Sprinter (21 days)

With this timeline, you'll build your RVP in the first 7 days and then spend the next 14 days promoting it. It's a bit more breathing room than the Weekend Warrior, but still fast-paced. You'll be working in focused bursts each week, with clear milestones to hit.

Option 3. The Steady Pacer (28 days)

This is the most relaxed of the three timelines, but still pretty quick by most standards. You'll build your RVP over the first 2 weeks, with a 1-week promotion buffer before launch. You'll be making steady progress via weekly milestones, with a bit more time to refine and polish your offer.

So, which timeline should you choose? Think of it like training for a race. Some people thrive on compressed prep times, using the pressure to sharpen their focus and build excitement. Others prefer a slightly longer runway, giving them time to build strength and endurance.

There's no one "right" answer. But, here's a key principle to keep in mind. Research has shown that hard goals with tight deadlines boost motivation and performance more than easy, open-ended goals. In other words, a little bit of positive stress can be a good thing.

So as you're considering your options, don't just default to the longest timeline. Pick the one that excites you and compels you to take focused action. A short deadline has a way of making your dream feel urgent and real.

Imagine telling your friends, "I'm launching my new program in just 14 days." Feel the adrenaline kick in? That's the power of a tight timeline. It takes your goal from someday to right now.

So which path calls to you? The Weekend Warrior, the Weekly Sprinter, or the Steady Pacer? Whichever you choose, know that you're setting yourself up for rapid learning and growth. By embracing a short timeline, you're not just validating your offer - you're validating your ability to make things happen. And that's a skill that will serve you well in all areas of life.

Today's Exercise: Choose Your Rapid Validation Timeline

Alright, it's time to take action! Let's do a quick exercise to help you choose your RVP timeline and make it real.

First, take a look at the three timeline options we just covered: the Weekend Warrior (14 days), the Weekly Sprinter (21 days), and the Steady Pacer (28 days). Think about your current schedule, your working style, and the type of offer you're creating. Which timeline resonates with you most?

Are you the type of person who thrives under intense pressure, or do you prefer a bit more breathing room? Do you have a relatively open schedule right now, or are you juggling a lot of commitments? Is your offer something that you can create quickly, or does it require more extensive development?

Take a few minutes to really consider which timeline feels like the best fit for you. Trust your gut - there's no wrong answer here.

Once you've chosen your timeline, it's time to make it real. Open up your calendar and start blocking out time to work on your RVP. If you chose the Weekend Warrior timeline, find a weekend where you can devote 2-3 full days to creating your offer. If you chose the Weekly Sprinter or Steady Pacer, block out a few hours each day or a couple of larger chunks each week.

Here's the key: treat these blocks of time as non-negotiable appointments with yourself. Just like you wouldn't skip out on a meeting with an important client, don't skip out on your RVP work sessions. Protect this time fiercely, and show up fully committed to making progress.

Finally, it's time to bring in some accountability. Share your chosen timeline and your scheduled work blocks with a friend, colleague, or mastermind partner. Ask them to check in with you regularly to make sure you're staying on track. Having someone else in your corner can be a huge motivator and can help you push through any rough patches.

And remember, this is just the beginning. Once you've completed your RVP, you'll have a wealth of learning and insight to build on.

You'll know what resonates with your audience, what falls flat, and what to double down on next. By choosing a short timeline and committing fully to the process, you're setting yourself up for rapid growth and success.

So take a deep breath, choose your timeline, and dive in. Your RVP adventure awaits!

Key Takeaways:

- Short validation timelines combat procrastination and perfectionism by creating positive pressure to act.

- Short deadlines shift focus to what's key. They encourage real-world testing over endless planning.

- Consciously choose a timeline for your RVP launch: 14, 21, or 28 days. Block out time and find an accountability partner. Commitment turns goals into results.

6

Pillar 2. Design (The Offer Clarity Grid)

Walt Disney knew how to captivate an audience. His animated films have delighted generations of children and adults. They have become cultural touchstones that have lasted. But what was the secret to his success?

As it turns out, Disney relied on a simple four-part story structure to craft his most beloved tales. His films include "Snow White and the Seven Dwarfs" and "The Lion King." Each follows a clear pattern: a hero with a goal, a problem in their way, a promise of change, and a path to get there.[7]

This structure may seem obvious in retrospect, but its power cannot be overstated. Disney broke complex narratives into key parts. This let them create simple but moving stories. He knew that audiences crave clarity most. They want to know what the hero wants. Also, they want to know what's stopping the hero and how they can overcome those obstacles to achieve their dreams.

The same principles apply when crafting an offer for your audience as a writer, coach, teacher or speaker. You might be writing a low-content book, creating a mini-course or bootcamp, or hosting a virtual workshop. In all cases, a clear structure is key. It helps you engage and persuade your audience to buy your products or services.

Like Disney's films, your offer needs similar elements. It must hook people at the start and get them excited to go on the journey with you. Just as Disney films did, you need an early emotional connection. This creates the dramatic tension that carries through the whole story. What shiny outcome can you hook their interest with? You can do this through your title, subtitle, and book description. What major problem do they currently have that is preventing them from getting what they want? What transformation can you confidently promise them that will change the trajectory of their life? And finally, what is the clear path you will guide them on to get from where they are now to where they want to go?

If Walt Disney could use this timeless formula to create cinematic magic, imagine what it could do for your business.

The Offer Clarity Grid

You're browsing through a sea of online courses, trying to find one that will help you achieve your goals. You come across a course that promises to teach you everything you need to know about your topic of interest. Excited, you dive in, only to find yourself drowning in a deluge of information. The course is packed with content, but there's no clear structure or path to follow. You feel overwhelmed, confused, and frustrated.

Sound familiar? It's a common trap that many course creators, coaches, and authors fall into. They think that more is better, so they cram as much information as possible into their offers. But here's the thing: people don't just want information. They want transformation.

Think about it. When you buy a book, course, or coaching program, what are you really looking for? You're not just looking for a bunch of facts and figures. You're looking for a clear path to achieve a specific outcome. You want someone to guide you from where you are now to where you want to be.

That's where the offer clarity grid comes in. By using this simple, structured framework, you can design your offer around a clear outcome. You don't overwhelm your audience. You give them a few key steps. These steps guide them to the transformation they desire.

Imagine going on a hike. You have a destination in mind, but you don't have a map or a guide. You're left to wander aimlessly through the wilderness, hoping that you'll eventually stumble upon your goal. It's frustrating and exhausting, and chances are, you'll give up before you ever reach your destination.

Now, imagine going on that same hike with a clear map and a knowledgeable guide. They lead you down a well-marked path, pointing out landmarks and giving you tips along the way. You know exactly where you're going and how to get there. The journey is still challenging, but it's also rewarding and achievable.

That's the power of a well-structured offer. By breaking your process down into clear, actionable steps, you give your audience the map and the guidance they need to achieve their goals. Instead of feeling overwhelmed and confused, they feel empowered and motivated.

So, if you want to create an offer that truly resonates with your audience, don't just dump information on them. Use the offer clarity grid to design a clear path to transformation. Your audience will thank you for it.

The offer clarity grid is a powerful tool that can help you create compelling offers that truly resonate with your audience. Follow these four steps. They will help you design an offer. The offer will provide a clear path to change and real value to your customers.

The Offer Clarity Grid

Plot	Problem	Promise
What does the hero want?	What's stopping them?	What can you help them achieve?

Path
What are the 3-7 steps to get there?

Step 1. Plot - What does the hero want?

Before you start creating your offer, you need to have crystal clarity on the end result your audience desires. What are their goals related to your topic? What transformation do they want to achieve?

Think of it like a GPS. Just as a GPS needs a clear destination to map out a route, your offer needs a well-defined outcome to build towards. Without a specific endpoint in mind, you'll be driving around in circles, wasting time and energy.

So, get specific. What transformation do you help people achieve? Is it more income, better health, and improved relationships? Whatever it is, build everything in your offer around that specific outcome.

Step 2. Problem - What's stopping them?

Once you know where your audience wants to go, you need to understand what's holding them back. What are the key problems they face in achieving their goals?

Remember, people don't buy products or services just for the sake of it. They invest in solutions to their problems. So, if you want to create a compelling offer, you need to articulate the specific challenges your audience is facing.

How do you figure out what those problems are? Ask them! Survey your audience with questions like, "What is your single biggest challenge when it comes to [your topic]?" Collect their answers and look for patterns. What problems come up over and over again?

Once you have a clear understanding of the problems your audience is facing, use that information to frame your offer as the solution they need. Show how your product or service addresses those challenges. Put this in your marketing materials.

Step 3. Promise - What can you help them achieve?

Now that you know where your audience wants to go and what's holding them back, it's time to make a promise. What transformation can you confidently offer them?

Your promise should be clear, concise, and compelling - ideally 10 words or less. It should summarize the specific outcome your audience can expect to achieve by investing in your offer.

Take Marie Forleo's "B-School" program, for example. Her promise is simple yet powerful: "Turn your business into a force for good and fuel your higher purpose." In just a few words, she shows the change her program provides. It brings not just money but the power to do good.

A great promise like this helps sell your offer and keeps you focused as you create it. Everything in your product or service should be designed to deliver on that key promise.

Step 4. Path - What are the 3-7 steps to get there?

Finally, you need to provide your audience with a clear path to achieve the transformation you've promised. Break your process down into a few simple, easy-to-follow steps that guide them from where they are now to where they want to be.

As Albert Einstein famously said, "If you can't explain it simply, you don't understand it well enough." Your job as the expert is to take your knowledge and experience and distill it down into a step-by-step roadmap that anyone can follow.

Aim for 3-7 steps, max. Any more than that, and you risk overwhelming your audience. Remember, people are looking for simplicity and clarity, not complexity.

Breaking your offer into clear steps gives your audience confidence. It also motivates them to take action. They know exactly what they need to do to achieve their goals, and they have a trusted guide (that's you!) to lead the way.

Today's Exercise: Complete to Offer Clarity Grid

Alright, it's time to put the offer clarity grid into action! This is where the rubber meets the road. You've learned the four key components of a compelling offer - plot, problem, promise, and path. Now, it's time to apply them to your own business.

Here's what I want you to do. Take the next 10-15 minutes and follow these four simple steps to outline your offer using the offer clarity grid.

Step 1: Write down the key outcome or transformation your offer helps people achieve. What specific result do you help your audience reach? Is it losing 20 pounds, doubling their income, finding their soulmate? Get crystal clear on the end goal.

Step 2: List out the 3-5 biggest problems or challenges your audience faces in achieving that outcome. What's holding them back from getting what they want? Is it a lack of time, lack of knowledge, or limiting beliefs? Brainstorm all the obstacles standing in their way.

Step 3: Draft a clear, compelling promise that encapsulates the results you provide. Remember, keep it short and sweet - 10 words or less. This is the hook that will grab your audience's attention and make them want to learn more.

Step 4: Outline the 3-7 steps you guide people to take to go from problem to outcome. What's the roadmap you provide? Break it down into clear, actionable steps that your audience can follow to achieve the transformation you've promised.

Don't overthink it. Just get your ideas down on paper. You can always refine and polish it later. The key is to start putting the pieces together and getting a clear picture of what your offer looks like.

And don't worry if it feels a little messy or incomplete at first. Building a compelling offer takes time and iteration. The offer clarity grid is a tool to help you get started, but it's not a magic bullet. You'll likely need to tweak and adjust as you go based on feedback from your audience.

But by taking the time to go through this exercise, you're already ahead of the game. You're creating an offer that is thoughtful, strategic, and designed to deliver real value to your customers. And that's what sets you apart from all the noise and clutter out there.

So grab a pen and paper (or open up a blank document on your computer) and get to work! Your dream offer awaits.

Key Takeaways:

- Using a clear offer framework like the Offer Clarity Grid enables you to create compelling, persuasive offers that sell.

- Get crystal clarity on the problems your audience faces and the outcomes they want before creating your offer. Build everything around, guiding them to transformation.

- Distill your offer into a concise promise and 3-7 step path from problem to outcome. Make your offer as simple and easy to understand as possible.

7

Creating Your Low-Content Book (Writers)

I t was the early 1700s in colonial America, and a young Benjamin Franklin was trying to make a name for himself as a writer and thinker. But he's got a problem. Nobody knows who he is, and he doesn't have the money or connections to get his ideas out there. Sound familiar?

So what does he do? He gets creative. In 1732, Franklin published the first edition of "Poor Richard's Almanack". He used the pseudonym Richard Saunders. It's a small, cheap book filled with practical advice, witty sayings, and entertaining stories. Kind of like the colonial version of a low-content book.

And guess what? It's a hit. People love it. They start quoting Poor Richard's wisdom in their daily lives. They eagerly await each new edition. Slowly but surely, Benjamin Franklin builds a reputation as a man of insight and intelligence.[8]

Here's the kicker: "Poor Richard's Almanack" wasn't a grand philosophy or groundbreaking science book. It was a simple, accessible way for Franklin to test his ideas, connect with readers, and establish his brand. All without risking a huge amount of time or money.

So why am I telling you this story? Because the same principle applies to writers today. In a world where anyone can publish a book, it's harder than ever to stand out and get noticed. But by using low-content books strategically, you can validate your niche. You can also build an audience and set yourself up for long-term success. Just like Ben Franklin did almost 300 years ago.

In this chapter, we're going to dive deep into the power of low-content books as a tool for writers. We'll explore why they work, how to create them quickly and easily, and how to use them to skyrocket your writing career. Get ready to take some notes because this could be the secret weapon you've been looking for.

How to Create Your Low Content Book

So you've got a brilliant idea for a book. A story that's been burning inside you for years, or a topic you're passionate about sharing with the world. You pour your heart and soul into writing. You spend many late nights hunched over your keyboard. You sacrifice time with friends and family to bring your vision to life.

Finally, after months (or maybe even years) of hard work, you type that last sentence, breathe a sigh of relief, and hit "publish." This is it. Your masterpiece is finally out there for the world to see.

But then... crickets. No sales. No reviews. No recognition. Just a sinking feeling that maybe, just maybe, you wasted all that time and effort on something nobody actually wanted to read.

It's a gut-punching realization, but here's the hard truth: most aspiring writers put the cart before the horse. They spend forever creating a full-length book without ever stopping to validate their idea or see if there's a market for it. They assume that if they build it, readers will come.

But that's a dangerous assumption. More often than not, it leads to disappointment, frustration, and books that never find their audience. You pour your blood, sweat, and tears into a project, only to watch it languish in obscurity.

So what's the solution? How can you avoid this painful scenario and set yourself up for success?

Here's a radical idea: start small.

Before you invest months or years into writing your magnum opus, test the waters with a low-content book. It's a low-risk, high-reward way to validate your niche, get feedback from real readers, and build momentum for your writing career.

Think about it. With a low-content book, you can:

- Create something valuable in a fraction of the time it takes to write a full book

- Get your work out there quickly and start building an audience

- Gather real-world data on what resonates with readers (and what doesn't)

- Build your confidence and skills as a writer and publisher

- Lay the groundwork for bigger, more ambitious projects down the road

Best of all, you can do it without breaking the bank or putting all your eggs in one basket. If your low-content book takes off, great! You've got proof of concept and a built-in audience for your next book. If it doesn't, no worries. You can pivot, adjust, and try again without losing months or years of your life.

So, if you're an aspiring writer with a big idea, don't make the mistake of jumping straight into the deep end. Dip your toes in the water with a low-content book first. Test, validate, and refine your concept. And then, when you're ready, dive in with confidence, knowing that you've got a winning formula for success.

Creating a low-content book can be a fast, effective way to serve your audience and generate income. By following a few key steps, you can develop a valuable resource that showcases your expertise and helps you stand out in your niche.

Step 1. Choose Your Book Type and Niche

Like a chef, select the right ingredients. Choose the type of low-content book and niche that best serves your audience. Will you create a workbook to accompany your signature course? A journal to help your coaching clients reflect on their progress? A planner tailored to busy moms in your community?

- Decide if you'll create a workbook, journal, planner, or a combination

- Consider your target audience and their needs

- Brainstorm at least 5 topic ideas that align with your niche and expertise

Take time to brainstorm ideas and get clear on what your people want and need. The more specific you can get, the better. Clarity on your book type and niche lays the foundation for a focused, valuable resource.

Step 2. Set Up Your Book Template

Using a tool like Canva, set up a template that includes all the essential pages and elements. Consider your book cover, welcome page, copyright notice, and table of contents. Customize your fonts, colors, and graphics to create a cohesive look that reflects your unique brand style. An intentional book template ensures a professional, polished final product.

- Use Canva or another design tool to create your book template

- Include essential pages like the cover, welcome, copyright, and table of contents

- Customize your design with fonts, colors, and graphics that reflect your brand

As Steve Jobs once said, "Design is not just what it looks like and feels like. Design is how it works." Thoughtful design is essential for creating a book that not only looks great but also functions well for your readers.

Step 3. Develop Your Content Pages

As you develop your book's core content pages, aim for a clean, inviting design that's easy to recreate. For a journal, this might include a daily prompt, space for reflection, and an inspiring quote. For a workbook, you might have a chapter summary, exercises, and reflection questions. Use minimal colors to keep printing costs down and ensure your book is easy to use. Well-designed, repeatable content pages are key to an engaging, cost-effective book.

- Create master layouts for core content pages (e.g., daily

prompts, chapter summaries)

- Keep the design clean, inviting, and easy to replicate

- Use minimal colors to keep printing costs down

Step 4. Generate Valuable Content

A 2021 study by Cornell University found that people are more likely to engage with content that is clear, concise, and relevant to their needs. As you generate your book's content, keep your target reader front and center. What questions do they have? What challenges are they facing? What insights or inspiration do they need?

- Write prompts, summaries, exercises, and reflections that serve your audience

- Consider using AI tools like Magi to spark ideas and streamline the writing process

- Ensure all content aligns with your voice, brand, and objectives

Aim to create prompts, summaries, exercises, and reflections. They should provide real value and help your readers reach their goals. AI tools like Magi can be a great way to spark ideas and streamline the writing process. Just be sure to review and edit all content to ensure it aligns with your authentic voice and brand. Providing targeted, valuable content will keep your readers engaged and coming back for more.

Step 5. Refine and Polish Your Book

As a sculptor refines their work to reveal the masterpiece within, review and refine your book to create a valuable resource. Go through each page with a fine-tooth comb, checking for typos, formatting issues, and overall clarity. Preview your book to ensure the pages are in the right order and everything looks just right.

- Review each page for errors, formatting issues, and overall clarity

- Preview your book to ensure proper page order and a polished final product

- Consider asking a friend or professional to proofread for an extra set of eyes

Don't be afraid to ask for help in this process. A fresh set of eyes can catch things you might miss. Consider asking a friend or hiring a professional proofreader to review your work. Thorough review and refinement are essential. They make a professional, high-quality book.

Creating a low-content book is a powerful way to serve your audience and grow your business. Follow these steps. Focus on providing real value. Then, you can make a resource that positions you as an expert and helps you stand out in your niche.

So what are you waiting for? Get started today and see where this exciting journey takes you. With a little creativity and hard work, you might just surprise yourself with what you can create. Your perfect low-content book is waiting to be born!

Today's Exercise: Brainstorming Your Low Content Book Ideas

It's time to put all this theory into practice. Grab a notebook or a whiteboard. Or use whatever gets your creative juices flowing. Let's start brainstorming some low-content book ideas for your niche.

Set a timer for 15 minutes, and challenge yourself to come up with at least 3-5 ideas. Don't worry about making them perfect - this is just a brainstorming session. The goal is to get your ideas out of your head and onto the page.

For each idea, ask yourself:

1. Who is my target reader? Get specific - what are their pain points, their goals, their interests? The more you can drill down into who you're creating for, the better.

2. What key value will this book provide? Will it help them solve a problem, achieve a goal, or explore a topic they're passionate about? Your book should have a clear value proposition that speaks directly to your target reader's needs.

3. How can I create this content quickly? Remember, the goal with low-content books is to minimize your upfront investment and get your work out there fast. Think about templates, tools, or resources you could use to streamline the creation process.

For example, let's say you're in the personal finance niche. Here are a few low-content book ideas you might come up with:

- A budgeting workbook for recent college grads struggling

with student loan debt

- A savings tracker for couples saving for their first home

- A debt payoff planner for people looking to get out of credit card debt

For each idea, you'd name the target reader and the key problem the book addresses. You'd also explain how to create the content quickly using existing templates or resources.

The beauty of this exercise is that it gets you thinking creatively about how you can serve your audience in small, focused ways. You don't have to create a 300-page masterpiece right out of the gate. You can start small, test the waters, and see what resonates with your readers.

So go ahead - set that timer, grab your brainstorming tools, and let the ideas flow. You never know what brilliant low-content book concept might emerge from this simple 15-minute exercise. And who knows - it might just be the thing that kickstarts your writing career and helps you build a loyal following in your niche.

Key Takeaways:

- Low-content books are a fast, low-cost way for writers to test their ideas and get real market feedback.

- Focusing your low-content book on a specific niche allows you to deliver targeted value and start building an audience.

- Making and publishing low-content books builds your skills, credibility, and platform. It sets you up for success as an author.

8
Developing Your Mini-Course (Teachers)

Music publishers faced a daunting challenge in the early 1900s. No radio. No TV. No Spotify. Just the challenging task of promoting new tunes to the masses with nothing more than paper and pianos.

Pushing new songs was painfully expensive and slow. Most heard a melody once and quickly forgot it. Sheet music sat unsold, collecting dust. What was a publisher to do?

Enter the "song pluggers." Part pianist, part traveling salesman, these unsung heroes of the early music industry had one job: give people a taste of the latest tunes. Armed with a grin and a gig book, they'd travel the country setting up "mini concerts" in public spaces. A hotel lobby here, a theater entrance there. Wherever folks gathered, the pluggers were there, tickling the ivories.

And here's the genius part: They'd only play 20 seconds of each song. Just enough to get the melody stuck in your mind. Just enough to leave you wanting more. Then they'd pack up their piano and vanish, leaving a trail of catchy tunes in their wake.

The result? A surge in sheet music sales. The "mini-concerts" wormed earworms deep into the minds of the masses. And once a tune took hold, people raced to buy the sheet music so they could play it themselves.[9]

The song pluggers discovered a powerful principle: A well-crafted preview can capture attention and drive demand - fast. And that same principle is the key to quickly launching your first online course.

Just like a 20-second song preview, a short "mini-course" gives your audience a taste of what you offer. A handful of videos, each just a few minutes long. Laser-focused on solving one specific problem. It's not the whole symphony - just the hook. The core value, concentrated.

And just like those song previews, a strong mini-course leaves people wanting more. It provides a quick win, a burst of success. And once they've had that taste, they're primed to buy your full program.

In this chapter, I'll show you how to rapidly create your own "mini-course" and get it up for sale lightning fast. We'll cover:

- The power of solving a single, specific problem

- How to structure your mini-course as a series of quick, actionable steps

- The key to positioning your mini-course as an irresistible "before and after" transformation

- A 15-minute exercise to choose your mini-course topic and get started this week

By the end of this chapter, you'll have a simple, proven process for going from idea to offer in record time. So grab a seat, and let's dive in. Class is about to begin.

The One Mistake That Stops Most Course Creators in Their Tracks

So you're excited to create your first online course. Congrats! Teaching what you know is one of the most satisfying and profitable ways to share your gifts with the world.

But where most new course creators go wrong is when they set out to build the Ultimate Mega Course. You know, that hulking beast of a program that covers every conceivable aspect of the topic. The one that takes months or even years to create. The one that sucks up every spare moment and leaves you wondering if you'll ever actually get to launch the damn thing.

I call this the "Sistine Chapel Trap." Instead of focusing on creating a simple, useful product, you get seduced by the idea of painting a masterpiece. A magnum opus that will stand the test of time and cement your status as the ultimate authority on the subject.

And hey, I get it. It's natural to want your course to be "definitive." To imagine students bowing at your brilliance as you reveal secret after secret. But here's the hard truth: trying to be too comprehensive is the enemy of actually launching the thing.

When you set out to cover everything, you quickly get overwhelmed by the sheer volume of content you could include. You start second-guessing yourself, wondering what to put in and what to leave out. You fall into an endless loop of planning, researching, and outlining, never quite feeling ready to start putting pixels on the screen.

Weeks turn to months. Your enthusiasm fades. The project starts to feel more like a burden than a joy. You tell yourself you just need a bit more time to "get it right." But deep down, you know the real issue: you've bitten off more than you can chew.

Here's a liberating truth: your course doesn't need to be the end-all, be-all epic on the topic. It doesn't need to answer every question or cover every scenario. Thoroughness is not the goal - transformation is.

Your job is not to cram your customers' heads full of information. It's to help them solve a specific problem or achieve a specific goal. And the more tightly you can focus your course on that singular outcome, the easier it will be to create and the more valuable it will be to your customers.

Think about it this way: when you have a leaky faucet, you don't need a plumber to explain the entire history and theory of indoor plumbing. You just need them to show up and fix the leak.

Your course is the same. Customers aren't coming to you for an exhaustive brain dump. They're coming to you for a targeted solution to a pressing problem. They want to get from A to B, not explore every side road and scenic overlook along the way.

The power of the mini-course is that it forces you to zero in on delivering a single, specific transformation. You focus on getting customers from A to B, not A to Z. You cut out fluff, filler, and distractions. You hone in on the core steps they need to take to get one meaningful win.

This narrow focus makes your course infinitely easier to create because you're no longer trying to boil the ocean. It makes it far more valuable to your customers because every lesson is laser-targeted to help them get the result they came for.

So, as you set out to plan your mini-course, keep this mantra in mind: "one problem, one solution." Resist the temptation to expand your scope. Have the courage to keep it tight and focused. Your students (and your sanity) will thank you.

The 3 Keys to Crafting a Laser-Focused Mini-Course

Now that we've covered the power of keeping your course tightly focused. Let's dive into the step-by-step process for planning and outlining your mini-course. There are three key phases:

Step 1. Pick a Super Niche Topic

Broad is boring. The more narrowly you can define your course topic, the easier it will be to create and the more enticing it will be for your ideal customers.

For example, let's say you're a nutrition coach. Instead of creating a generic "Healthy Eating 101" course, zero in on a specific outcome like "7 Days to Kick Sugar Cravings." The more specific the promise, the more powerful the appeal.

A recent study of Udemy's top 1000 courses found that 80% focused on one specific skill. For example, "Mastering Python for Data Science" or "Watercolor Painting for Beginners." Niche courses trounce broad ones every time.

The takeaway? Customers don't pay for information - they pay for transformation. And the more specific and tangible that transformation is, the more excited they'll be to whip out their wallets. A tight promise trumps vague concepts every time.

Step 2. Think Steps, Not Information

Once you've nailed your specific topic, it's time to break it down into bite-sized steps. Because here's the thing: your customers don't just need to know what to do - they need to know how to do it.

Think of your course like a recipe. Giving students ingredients isn't enough. You need to walk them through the steps to combine the ingredients into a dish. "Step 1: Dice the onions" is a lot more helpful than "You'll need onions."

So as you outline your mini-course, think in terms of action steps, not just information. Aim for 3-8 brief, actionable steps, each of which will become a short video lesson.

For each step, ask yourself: "What does the customer need to do to move forward?" Not just "What do they need to know?" Remember, action engages while facts bore. The more you can break things down into clear, concrete steps, the more your students will actually implement what you teach.

Step 3. Create the Before & After

The most powerful way to position your mini-course is to paint a vivid "before and after" picture. You want to be crystal clear on the transformation your course will provide.

Ask yourself: How will customers feel before taking your course? Frustrated? Overwhelmed? Stuck? Now, how will they feel after completing it? Confident? Relieved? Empowered?

As copywriting expert Samuel Hulick puts it, "People don't buy products, they buy better versions of themselves." Your job is to vividly describe the "better version" your course will help them become.

For example, let's say you're teaching a course on public speaking. The "before" state might be feeling anxious and avoiding speaking opportunities. The "after" state is feeling poised and confident, able to captivate any room.

In your course marketing, you'd want to agitate the pain of the "before" state and then promise the pleasure of the "after." For example:

"Tired of breaking into a cold sweat every time you're asked to speak up in meetings? Imagine being able to stand up and share your ideas with confidence and poise. You would leave your colleagues impressed and inspired. That's exactly what you'll be able to do after completing my "Confident Public Speaking Mini-Course."

The key takeaway? Features tell, but benefits sell. Instead of just rattling off a list of what your course covers, focus on the real-world impact it will have. How will your customer's day-to-day life be better as a result of taking your course? The more viscerally you can paint that picture, the more irresistible your offer will become.

Today's Exercise: Find Your Mini-Course Sweet Spot

Alright, now it's time to take what you've learned and apply it to your own course creation process. Don't worry, this won't be some marathon brainstorming session that leaves you more overwhelmed than when you started. We're going to keep things focused and actionable, just like a good mini-course should be.

Here's your 15-minute exercise:

Brainstorm three potential mini-course topics. These should be tightly focused, specific outcomes you could help your customers achieve. Not broad overviews, but targeted solutions to pressing problems. Aim for topics you could reasonably cover in 3-7 short video lessons.

For each potential topic, jot down:

- The specific problem it solves. What pain point or frustration will this course alleviate for your customers? The more vividly you can articulate the problem, the more compelling your course will be.

- The 3-7 key steps you'd teach. Remember, think in terms of action steps, not just information. What will customers need to do to get from A to B? Break it down into clear, bite-sized chunks.

- The before and after transformation. How will customers feel before taking your course? How will they feel after completing it? What tangible results will they be able to achieve? Paint a vivid picture of the transformation your course provides.

Look over your 3 potential topics and pick the one that feels most exciting and energizing to you. Which one lights you up and gets your creative juices flowing? Which one do you feel most uniquely qualified to teach?

Take that winning topic and start outlining your mini-course in more detail. Flesh out each of the 3-7 key steps with bullet points of what you'll cover. Jot down any specific examples, stories, or exercises you might want to include.

The goal here is to strike while the iron is hot and make tangible progress on your course plan. You don't need to script out every word, but you should end up with a clear, actionable outline that you can use as a roadmap for creating your course content.

And here's the beautiful thing: once you've completed this exercise, you'll be well on your way to having your first mini-course ready to launch. You'll have a narrow topic. You'll have a clear outline. You'll have a compelling transformation for your customers.

So don't get bogged down trying to plan out some epic magnum opus. Just carve out 15 minutes, grab a notebook or open up a fresh doc, and start brainstorming. The key is to take action and build momentum. Because the sooner you get that first mini-course out into the world, the sooner you can start making sales and changing lives.

You've got this. Now, let's get to work.

Key Takeaways:

- Creating a super-specific "mini-course" of 10 videos or less is often the fastest path to your first sale

- Organize your course around a series of actionable steps, not just information

- Sell the transformation. Get clear on the before and after, and focus your messaging on the benefits of the "after" state your course helps customers reach.

9

Structuring Your 4-Week Bootcamp (Coaches)

R amit Sethi has an idea for a course that teaches people how to earn an extra $1,000 a month. Exciting stuff, right? But here's the thing—it's 2009, and he doesn't want to spend countless hours creating the course only to hear crickets when he launches. Talk about a waste of time and energy.

So what does Ramit do? He decides to sell the course to a small test group before he even creates the full program. Genius move. By doing this, he's able to validate that people actually want what he's offering. And not just that - he can gather valuable feedback from the test group to make the course even better.

Fast forward a bit, and Ramit's "Earn1K" course is a smashing success. People are raving about it, and the full launch goes off without a hitch. All because he took the time to validate his idea and get feedback from real people before diving in headfirst.[10]

And that, my friend, is the power of selling before you create. It's a simple concept, but it can make all the difference in the world when it comes to launching a successful product or service. Just like Ramit sold his course to a test group before creating the full program, you can do the same with your coaching offer.

By pre-selling your bootcamp to a small group of beta customers, you get to check your idea. You can make sure there's really demand for what you're offering. Also, you can use the feedback and insights from your beta group. Use them to refine and improve your boot-camp before launching it to a wider audience.

It's a win-win situation. You get to test the waters and make sure you're on the right track. Your beta customers get to be part of something exclusive. They provide valuable input that shapes the final product. When you launch to a broader audience, you'll have the confidence and social proof to back up your offer.

The Beta Bootcamp Blueprint: Get Paid to Create Your Coaching Program

Let me ask you something. When you're creating an online course or coaching program, what's your usual approach? Most people do this. They spend months holed up, pouring their heart into creating the perfect program. You're excited about your ideas and can't wait to share them with the world.

But here's the problem: you're doing it all in isolation, without any feedback from the people who actually matter - your customers. You're investing a ton of time and resources into something that you *think* people want, but you don't actually know for sure.

And then, when you finally launch your program, you're met with a harsh reality. Crickets. Tumbleweeds. Maybe a few pity purchases from your mom and best friend. Ouch.

The truth is that creating your whole program ahead of time is a risky move. You're essentially gambling with your time and energy, hoping that people will be willing to pay for what you've created. But what if they don't? What if you've completely missed the mark and created something that doesn't resonate with your audience at all?

But, by making your program in a vacuum, you're missing a big chance. You're missing the chance to tailor your content to the needs and questions of your ideal customers. You're just guessing at what they want rather than actually listening to them and creating something that truly serves them.

So, what's the solution? It's simple: pre-sell a 4-week group coaching bootcamp to a small beta cohort first. This is a game-changer, my friend.

By pre-selling your program, you're able to validate that there's actually demand for what you're offering. You're not just creating and hoping people will buy it. You're getting real, paying customers to sign up before you've even created the full program.

And the best part? These beta customers become your own personal focus group. You get to hear their feedback, questions, and concerns. You will gather insights that you can use to refine your program before launching it to a wider audience.

Plus, by charging for your beta program, you're essentially getting paid to create your course content. How cool is that? Your beta customers are funding your course development rather than you having to invest a ton of time and money upfront.

Alright, let's dive into the nitty-gritty of how to structure and sell your 4-week group coaching bootcamp. Here are the key steps to follow:

Step 1. Define Your Bootcamp Topic and Promises

First things first - you need to get crystal clear on what your boot-camp is all about. What specific problem are you solving for your customers? What transformation will they achieve by the end of the

4 weeks? And what's the format - are we talking 4 live Zoom sessions, or something else?

Think of it like planning a trip. Before you start booking flights and hotels, you need to decide on your destination. Where do you want to go, and what do you want to experience when you get there? The same goes for your bootcamp. Nail down that topic and promise, and everything else will fall into place.

Remember: a clear bootcamp topic and promise are the foundation for all your messaging. They also guide curriculum development. Get this right, and the rest will be a whole lot easier.

Step 2. Outline Your 4-Week Curriculum at a High Level

Now that you know where you're headed, it's time to map out the route. What key topics, lessons, and activities will you cover each week? They will help your customers achieve the promised transformation.

Here's a pro tip: start with the end in mind. What do you want your customers to walk away with by the end of the bootcamp? Work backwards from there to create an outline of what you'll cover each week. And make it enticing - this is what you'll be sharing on your sales page to get people excited about signing up.

Remember what Stephen Covey said: "Begin with the end in mind." Reverse-engineer your bootcamp curriculum. Then, you'll be well on your way to creating something truly valuable for your customers.

Step 3: Set Your Price and Limit Spots to Create Urgency

Okay, let's talk money. How much should you charge for your beta bootcamp? The key is to find that sweet spot - a price that feels like an "easy yes" for your customers but still requires them to have some skin in the game.

And here's a little psychology trick for you: limit the number of spots available. Scarcity and urgency are powerful motivators. When something is in limited supply, people perceive it as more valuable.

In fact, a 2020 study by researchers at Carnegie Mellon University found that consumers saw products as more valuable. This was when the products were framed as scarce or limited. So don't be afraid to cap your bootcamp at a certain number of spots - it could be the very thing that pushes people to take action and sign up.

Step 4: Deliver Your Live 4-Week Bootcamp, Adapting As You Go

Alright, you've sold your bootcamp and it's time to deliver! Host your weekly group coaching sessions via Zoom. Guide your customers through the activities and discussions you've planned.

But here's the thing - you have to be ready to adapt on the fly. Pay attention to the questions your customers are asking, the challenges they're facing, and the aha moments they're having. These insights are pure gold, and they'll help you refine your bootcamp for future iterations.

Think of it like leading a guided tour. You have a planned itinerary, but sometimes, the best experiences happen when you take a little detour based on what the group is interested in. The same goes for your bootcamp. Be willing to adjust based on what your customers need. Then, you'll create a richer experience for everyone.

Step 5: Seek Feedback and Testimonials from Your Beta Customers

Last but not least, don't forget to gather feedback from your beta customers. This is your chance to find out what worked, what didn't, and what you can improve for next time.

Collect qualitative feedback (open-ended comments and suggestions). And if you can get some video testimonials, even better - there's nothing quite like hearing someone rave about your bootcamp in their own words.

So there you have it - the key steps to structuring and selling your 4-week group coaching bootcamp. It's not always easy, but trust me - the payoff is worth it. When you see your customers achieving those changes and praising you, you'll know you've made something truly valuable. And that's what it's all about, right?

Today's Exercise: Design Your 4-Week Bootcamp

Alright, it's time to get those creative juices flowing! Let's dive into a little brainstorming exercise that will help you come up with some killer ideas for your own 4-week group coaching bootcamp.

First things first - set aside 10-15 minutes for this. Turn off those pesky notifications, put your phone on silent, and find a quiet space where you can really focus.

Now, grab a pen and paper (or your favorite note-taking app) and start jotting down some ideas. Here are a few questions to get you started:

- What topics do people frequently come to you for advice on?

Maybe you're the go-to person in your group for social media tips. Or, perhaps you're always fielding questions about how to change careers.

- What transformation could you help a small group achieve in just 4 weeks with a structured program and some live support? Could you guide them through creating their first online course from start to finish? Or maybe you could help them develop a foolproof system for meal planning and prep so they can finally stick to their healthy eating goals.

Don't censor yourself - just let the ideas flow. Aim for 3-5 solid topic ideas that you could potentially turn into a bootcamp.

Got your list? Awesome. Now, take a look at those topics and choose the one that lights you up the most. The one that makes you feel excited and energized just thinking about it.

Once you've got your top pick, it's time to craft a compelling title and subheading. This is where you really want to speak to your ideal customer's pain points and the transformation they're craving.

For example, let's say your bootcamp topic is "How to Create Your First Online Course in Just 4 Weeks." Your title and subheading might look something like this:

"From Idea to Income: Launch Your Online Course in 4 Weeks Flat"

Subtitle: Stop procrastinating. Start profiting from your expertise. Take this step-by-step bootcamp for first-time course creators."

The title and subheading clearly show the customer's problem. They are procrastination and wanting to profit from their expertise. They also show the promised result: launching an online course in just 4 weeks. That's the goal here.

So take a crack at drafting a title and subheading for your chosen bootcamp topic. Experiment with different words and angles. Do this until you find something that feels very compelling. It should speak directly to your ideal customer.

And remember - this is just a brainstorming exercise. Don't put too much pressure on yourself to come up with the "perfect" idea right out of the gate. The goal here is simply to get your creative wheels turning and start exploring some possibilities.

Who knows - you might just stumble upon the bootcamp idea that changes everything for you and your business. So have fun with it, and happy brainstorming!

Key Takeaways:

- Selling your bootcamp first shows demand. It also gives insights and funds development. It all happens before making the full program.

- Limit spots and price strategically to create urgency. Deliver live to adapt on the go.

- Refine your offering based on beta feedback and testimonials. Iterate based on real customer experience.

10

Planning Your Virtual Workshop (Speakers)

C lose your eyes and imagine this: It's the 1950s in Chicago, and a bold new experiment in education is taking the city by storm. No more stuffy classrooms or boring lectures. No more battling traffic or rushing to make it to class on time. Instead, thousands of students are learning from their own living rooms. They can do this thanks to a pioneering program called the TV College.

A student settles into her favorite armchair, notepad, and pencil ready. She tunes in to the designated channel, and suddenly, the familiar face of her professor appears on the screen. But this is no ordinary lecture. The instructor is lively and engaging. They use dynamic visuals and clear explanations. These seem tailor-made for television.

The TV College, launched by Chicago's public colleges, was a game-changer. It brought education to the masses in a whole new way, breaking down barriers of access and opportunity. But it also faced a daunting challenge: How do you keep students engaged when they're not in the same room as their teacher and classmates?

The answer lies in the art of crafting compelling, interactive learning experiences. The instructors at the TV College couldn't rely on the usual tricks of the trade - no eye contact, no reading the room, no live Q&A. Instead, they had to get creative.

They used vibrant graphics and demonstrations to bring abstract concepts to life. They broke complex topics down into digestible chunks, perfect for the shorter attention spans of home viewers. They infused their presentations with personality and humor. This forged a connection with their unseen audience. In short, they mastered the art of engaging remote students. This skill is more important than ever in the age of virtual workshops and online learning.[11]

So what can we learn from the intrepid educators of the TV College? Their story reminds us that engaging virtual learners is all about adapting our approach to suit the medium. It's about being dynamic, visual, and relatable. It's about breaking free from the limits of traditional teaching. It's about getting creative in how we connect with our audience.

As we dive into the world of virtual workshops, let's keep the lessons of the TV College close at hand. Because if they could captivate thousands of students through the tiny screens of 1950s televisions, imagine what we can achieve with the interactive tools and technologies at our fingertips today.

The key to unlocking virtual workshops' full potential lies in crafting an agenda. It must keep participants engaged from start to finish. And that's exactly what we're going to explore in this chapter. So grab your notepad and get ready to channel your inner TV College professor - it's time to master the art of the virtual workshop agenda.

The Fatal Flaw of Most Virtual Workshops

You're excited to attend a virtual workshop on a topic you're passionate about. You clear your schedule, brew a fresh cup of coffee, and settle in at your computer, ready to learn. But as the minutes tick by, your enthusiasm starts to wane. The presenter drones on and on, reading from endless slides packed with tiny text. Your mind wanders, your attention drifts, and before you know it, you're struggling to keep your eyes open.

Sound familiar? It's a scenario that plays out all too often in the world of virtual workshops. And it's no wonder why.

The Perils of the Endless Lecture

Many well-intentioned presenters fall into a trap. They try to recreate the in-person workshop online. They figure, "Hey, I've got a captive audience for a few hours. I'll just lecture them nonstop, like I would in a classroom."

Big mistake.

Here's the thing: What works in person doesn't always translate to the virtual realm. When you're face-to-face with a presenter, there's a certain energy and connection that can sustain a longer lecture. But when you're staring at a screen, it's a whole different ballgame.

The Dreaded Zoom Fatigue

Ever heard of "Zoom fatigue"? It's that bone-deep exhaustion that sets in after hours of video calls and online meetings. And it's a very real phenomenon in the world of virtual workshops.

You're bombarded with non-stop talking heads and endless slides. Your brain quickly becomes overloaded. Your attention span dwindles, your eyes glaze over, and before you know it, you're mentally checked out. All that valuable information you were so excited to learn? It's going in one ear and out the other.

The result? The workshop falls flat. It leaves participants bored and disengaged. They question why they bothered to attend.

A Better Way Forward

But here's the good news: It doesn't have to be this way. A few simple tweaks to your virtual workshop agenda can make it engaging, interactive, and memorable. The tweaks work no matter how long the workshop is.

The key? Prioritizing interaction and variety.

Instead of droning on for hours, break your workshop up into bite-sized chunks. Aim for short, focused teaching segments of no more than 15-20 minutes at a time. Think of it like a delicious meal - you want to serve up a variety of flavors and textures to keep things interesting.

Between those teaching segments, mix in plenty of interactive elements. Encourage participants to apply what they're learning through hands-on exercises and activities. Spark lively discussions and Q&A sessions. And don't forget to sprinkle in some well-timed breaks to give everyone a chance to recharge and refocus.

The Magic Formula

So, what's the magic formula for a truly engaging virtual workshop? Here's a simple guideline to keep in mind:

Aim for a total workshop length of 2-4 hours, broken up into roughly one-hour segments. Within each segment, include a mix of:

- Short teaching bursts (15 minutes)

- Interactive exercises and activities (15 minutes)

- Q&A and/or breakout room discussion (15 minutes)

- Brief breaks (15 minutes)

By following this formula, you'll create a virtual workshop that's dynamic, engaging, and packed with value. Your participants will stay energized and focused. They will absorb key insights and use them right away.

So don't fall into the trap of the endless lecture. Embrace interaction and variety. Watch your virtual workshops soar. They will reach new heights of impact and effectiveness. Let's take a closer look at each segment.

The Five Key Steps to Virtual Workshop Success

Ready to craft a virtual workshop that truly engages and inspires? It all comes down to five key steps. Master these, and you'll be well on your way to delivering a workshop that packs a punch and leaves a lasting impact.

Step 1: Embrace the Power of "Bite-Sized" Teaching

Imagine you're a fitness trainer leading a high-energy workout class. You wouldn't have your participants do the same exercise for an hour straight, would you? Of course not! You'd mix things up. You'd alternate cardio, strength training, and stretching. This keeps them engaged and energized.

The same principle applies to virtual workshops. Don't bombard your audience with a marathon lecture. Instead, break your content into short, 15-minute segments. Think of each segment as a focused "sprint" that dives deep into a specific topic or skill.

By teaching in these short bursts, you maximize learning and minimize fatigue. Your participants stay alert, engaged, and ready to absorb new insights. It's a simple yet powerful way to keep the energy high and the momentum going.

Step 2: Bring Learning to Life with Applied Exercises

Ever heard the saying, "Practice makes perfect"? It's a cliché for a reason. When it comes to learning, there's no substitute for hands-on experience.

That's why, after each 15-minute teaching segment, it's crucial to give your participants a chance to apply what they've learned. Dedicate 10-15 minutes to an interactive exercise or activity that brings the concepts to life.

This isn't just a nice-to-have - it's backed by science. A 2014 study by Freeman et al. I found that active learning, like problem-solving and discussion, leads to better understanding. It's better than just passive listening.

So don't just tell your participants what to do - give them a chance to practice it for themselves. It might be a quick brainstorm, a mini-project, or a group discussion. These practical exercises will cement the learning and make it stick.

Step 3: Spark Lively Discussions with Q&A Sessions

Picture this: It's ancient Greece, and the great philosopher Socrates is engaging his students in a lively dialogue. He's not just lecturing them. He's asking thought-provoking questions, challenging their assumptions, and sparking new insights.

Fast forward a few thousand years and the power of questions remains just as potent. That's why, throughout your virtual workshop, it's essential to carve out dedicated time for Q&A sessions.

Aim to include a 15-minute Q&A block after every hour of content. This lets your participants ask clarifying questions. They can also share their own experiences and dive deeper into their favorite topics.

But Q&A isn't just a benefit for your audience - it's also an invaluable tool for you as the instructor. You can gauge their understanding by hearing from your participants. You can identify areas where they may struggle and adjust your approach on the fly. It's like having a real-time feedback loop that helps you tailor the workshop to their specific needs.

Step 4: Foster Connection and Collaboration with Breakout Rooms

One of the biggest challenges of virtual workshops is creating a sense of community and connection. When participants are scattered across different locations and time zones, it can be tough to foster that feeling of being "in it together."

That's where Zoom breakout rooms come in. Divide your participants into smaller groups. This creates chances for intimate discussions, teamwork, and peer learning.

As adult learning expert Jane Vella puts it, "The key to a great workshop is the right mix of content, activity, reflection, and interaction." Breakout rooms provide the essential interaction. They allow participants to learn from each other.

So don't be afraid to mix things up and send your participants into breakout rooms throughout the workshop. They are for quick icebreakers or more in-depth projects. These interactions build camaraderie and make learning feel personal and engaging.

Step 5: Give the Brain a Break

Last but not least, don't underestimate the power of a well-timed break. When you're in the thick of a multi-hour workshop, it can be tempting to plow through without coming up for air. But that's a recipe for burnout and disengagement.

The science is clear: Brief breaks are essential for maintaining focus and motivation. A 2011 study by Ariga and Lleras found that short breaks can reduce fatigue. They restore attention, helping participants stay sharp and engaged.

So make sure to schedule 10-15 minute breaks at least every hour. Encourage participants to step away from their screens, stretch their legs, grab a snack, or simply rest their eyes. These little moments of respite will help them recharge and come back ready to learn.

And there you have it - the five key steps to virtual workshop success. Break your content into bite-sized parts. Add applied exercises. Spark lively Q&As. Foster small group interactions. Give the brain a break. This will create a workshop that truly engages, inspires, and sticks with your participants. They'll remember it long after the final Zoom call.

Today's Exercise: Craft Your Engaging Workshop Agenda

Alright, it's time to put these principles into practice. Grab a pen and paper, or open up a fresh document on your computer. We're going to take the next 10-15 minutes to draft a high-level agenda for your own virtual workshop.

Don't worry about getting it perfect - this is just a starting point. The goal is to get your creative juices flowing. Start to see how you can structure your workshop for maximum engagement and impact.

Step 1: Determine Your Total Workshop Length

First things first: How long do you want your workshop to be? Aim for somewhere between 2-4 hours total. This is the sweet spot for most virtual workshops - long enough to dive deep into your content, but not so long that participants start to lose steam.

Step 2: Break It Down into Hourly Segments

Now that you have your total workshop length break it down into hourly segments. For example, if you're planning a 3-hour workshop, you'll have three one-hour segments to work with.

Step 3: Fill in Your Agenda Building Blocks

For each hourly segment, start slotting in the key building blocks of an engaging workshop:

- 1-3 content segments (15-20 minutes each)

- 1-3 interactive exercises or activities (10-15 minutes each)

- A 15-minute Q&A session

- A 10-15 minute break

Mix and match these elements in a way that feels natural and flows well with your content. Remember, variety is key - you want to keep things dynamic and engaging throughout the workshop.

Step 4: Rinse and Repeat

Once you've filled in your first hourly segment, repeat the process for the remaining segments. Again, don't get too bogged down in the details - this is just a high-level outline to give you a sense of the overall flow and structure.

Step 5: Stand Back and Admire Your Work

Take a step back and look at your completed agenda. How does it feel? Does it have a good mix of content, interaction, and breathing room? Are there any areas that feel too heavy or too light?

Don't be afraid to make tweaks and adjustments as needed. This is your workshop, and you know your content and audience best. Trust your instincts and create an agenda that feels authentic and engaging to you.

And there you have it - your first draft of an engaging virtual workshop agenda. It might not be perfect, but it's a great starting point. As you continue to refine and iterate, keep the key principles in mind. They are: short content, interactive exercises, lively Q&As, small group breakouts, and well-timed breaks.

With this foundation in place, you're on your way. You're making a virtual workshop that truly resonates and has a lasting impact. So go forth and create something amazing - your audience will thank you for it!

Key Takeaways:

- Vary activities and limit lectures to 15-minute segments to keep virtual workshops engaging.

- Applied exercises, Q&A, and small group breakouts create an interactive learning experience.

- Including breaks, each hour helps maintain energy and focus throughout multi-hour workshops.

11

Crafting Your Super Simple Sales Page

I t's 1984, and you're channel-surfing late at night. Suddenly, a charismatic pitchman appears on your screen, brandishing a gleaming set of knives. He then shows their sharpness by slicing through everything, from tomatoes to tin cans. He does this while praising the virtues of these miraculous blades. The Ginsu Knives infomercial changed how products were sold on TV. At the heart of this sales phenomenon was a simple but highly effective order form.

The Ginsu Knives campaign proved that you don't need a fancy, convoluted sales page to convince people to buy what you're offering. Their plain approach resulted in over 2 million knives sold. It showed the power of a well-crafted, no-nonsense sales message.[12]

That's what we'll focus on in this chapter. We'll make a simple but compelling sales page. It will help you validate your offer and start earning money. You can use it as a writer, coach, teacher, or speaker. You might be selling a low-content book, a mini-course, a group coaching program, or a virtual workshop. But, the principles are the same.

You need to cut through the noise, grab your audience's attention, and persuade them to take action. Just like the Ginsu Knives pitch, your sales page should be sharp, efficient, and impossible to ignore. So, let's dive in and learn how to craft a super simple sales page that will have your ideal customers eagerly reaching for their wallets!

Crafting Your Super Simple Sales Page (SSSP)

You've probably seen them before: those endless, scrolling sales pages. They go on forever and are packed with dense paragraphs, complicated jargon, and more bullet points than a military arsenal. It's like trying to navigate a maze, except instead of a prize at the end, you're left with a headache and a serious case of information overload.

Here's the thing: when it comes to sales pages, more isn't always better. In fact, those overly complicated, text-heavy monstrosities often do more harm than good. They fail to engage your target audience, and they don't clearly communicate the value of your offer. It's like trying to sell a gourmet meal by listing every ingredient in painful detail. By the time you get to the end, your customers have lost their appetite and moved on.

Complex sales pages are the equivalent of a boring, long-winded lecture. They overwhelm potential customers, making them feel like they're drowning in a sea of information. And what happens when people feel overwhelmed? They tune out, click away, and leave your page faster than you can say, "but wait, there's more!" High bounce rates and low conversion rates are the inevitable results of a sales page that's too complicated for its own good.

So, what's the alternative? To create a successful sales page, you need to focus on three key elements: simplicity, clarity, and engagement. Strip away all the fluff and get to the heart of what your target audience really wants. What are their pain points? What keeps them up at night? And most importantly, how can your offer solve their problems and make their lives better?

When you focus on these essential aspects, you'll be able to craft a sales page that truly resonates with your ideal customers. It's all about speaking their language. It's about addressing their needs and offering a clear, compelling solution. Think of it like a well-aimed arrow. You avoid scattering your message. Instead, you focus on hitting the bullseye. You aim to convince your audience to take action.

The 5-Step Formula to Creating a Sales Page in Under 60 Minutes

Alright, let's break down the five essential steps to crafting your super simple sales page:

Step 1. Identify the Pain Points

Imagine you're a doctor, and a patient comes to you with a set of symptoms. Before you can prescribe the right treatment, you need to understand exactly what's ailing them. The same principle applies to your sales page. Before you start writing, you need to identify your target audience and their specific pain points.

What keeps them up at night? What are the challenges they face day in and day out? Once you've clearly defined your target audience and their struggles, you can craft a message that speaks directly to their needs. Remember, the clearer you are about who you're talking to and what they're going through, the more compelling your sales page will be.

Step 2: Craft a Compelling Headline

As the legendary advertiser David Ogilvy once said, "On the average, five times as many people read the headline as read the body copy. When you have written your headline, you have spent eighty cents out of your dollar." In other words, your headline is the most important part of your sales page. It's the first thing people will see, and it's what will determine whether they keep reading or click away.

To create a headline that grabs attention and draws people in, focus on your audience's main problem. What's the biggest challenge they're facing? How can your offer help them overcome it? Craft a headline that speaks to your audience's needs. You'll have a much better chance of getting them to stick around and learn.

Step 3: Use the "Who, What, Why, How" Script

Once you've got your audience's attention with a great headline, it's time to structure your sales page. Do it in a way that's easy to follow and engaging. One simple but effective method is the "Who, What, Why, How" script, popularized by marketer Russell Brunson. Here's how it works:

1. Who are you, and why should your audience listen to you?

2. What is your offer, and what will it do for your audience?

3. Why should your audience care about your offer, and what makes it different from other solutions?

4. How can your audience get their hands on your offer, and what do they need to do next?

Organize your sales page content around these four key questions. This creates a logical flow. It keeps your audience engaged and moving toward the desired action.

Step 4: Highlight the Key Benefits

When it comes to selling your offer, features tell, but benefits sell. In other words, don't just list out the specs and details of your product or service. Instead, focus on the tangible outcomes and transformations your audience can expect. How will your offer make their lives better? What specific results can they achieve by working with you?

A 2012 study by the Harvard Business Review found that customers are more likely to purchase a product or service when the benefits are clearly communicated and aligned with their needs. So, don't be shy about spelling out exactly what your audience stands to gain. Paint a vivid picture of the success and relief they'll experience when they take you up on your offer.

Step 5: Include a Clear Call-to-Action

Finally, don't leave your audience hanging. Once you've got them excited about your offer, you need to guide them towards the next step. That's where your call-to-action (CTA) comes in. Think of it like a GPS. A GPS gives clear directions to reach a destination. Your CTA should give clear instructions on what your audience needs to do to get your offer.

Make your CTA specific, actionable, and impossible to miss. And remember, if you confuse, you lose. Keep it simple and straightforward so there's no question about what your audience needs to do next.

To sweeten the deal and boost conversions, consider adding a risk-reversal strategy. For example, you could add a money-back guarantee. This will make it easier for your audience to say "yes" to your offer, knowing that they have nothing to lose and everything to gain.

Today's Exercise: Your 60-Minute Super Simple Sales Page Challenge

Alright, let's dive into a practical, hands-on exercise that will help you craft your own super simple sales page. This is where the rubber meets the road, so get ready to put everything you've learned into action!

Objective: Create a draft of your super simple sales page using the "Who, What, Why, How" script and the strategies outlined in this chapter.

1. Set a timer for 60 minutes. This will help you stay focused and avoid getting bogged down in perfectionism.

2. Open a new document or grab a pen and paper. Whichever you prefer, make sure you have a space dedicated to this exercise.

3. Start by clearly defining your target audience. Who are they? What are their pain points and challenges? What keeps them up at night? Take 10 minutes to write out a detailed description of your ideal customer.

4. Next, spend 10 minutes brainstorming headline ideas. Remember, your headline should grab attention and speak directly to your audience's main problem. Don't worry about getting it perfect; the goal is to generate a list of potential options.

5. Now, it's time to fill in the "Who, What, Why, How" script. Take 10 minutes for each section:

- Who: Introduce yourself and establish your credibility. Why should your audience listen to you?

- What: Clearly explain your offer and what it will do for your audience.

- Why: Highlight the key benefits and outcomes of your offer. What makes it different from other solutions?

- How: Provide clear instructions on how your audience can get their hands on your offer. What do they need to do next?

6. Once you've completed the script, take 10 minutes to review and refine your work. Look for opportunities to simplify your language, clarify your message, and make your offer more compelling.

7. Finally, spend the last 10 minutes crafting a clear call-to-action. Also, think of risk-reversal ideas. How can you make it easy and low-risk for your audience to say "yes" to your offer?

By the end of this 60-minute challenge, you should have a solid draft of your super simple sales page. It may not be perfect, but that's okay! The goal is to get your ideas out of your head and onto the page. You can always refine and polish your work later.

Remember, crafting a compelling sales page is a skill that takes practice. Don't get discouraged if your first attempt feels a little clunky or awkward. The more you practice, the easier it will become. And who knows? With a little time and effort, you may just find yourself creating sales pages that would make even the Ginsu Knives pitchman proud!

Key Takeaways:

- Simplicity and clarity are key to a successful sales page.

- Identify your target audience's pain points and craft a compelling headline.

- Use the "Who, What, Why, How" script to structure your content.

- Highlight benefits, include a clear CTA, and offer a risk-reversal strategy.

12

Pillar 3. Deploy (Your RVP Launch Plan)

Ty Warner had a simple idea. In the early 1990s, he created a line of small, cute stuffed animals filled with plastic pellets. They were nothing revolutionary, but Warner saw potential. He named them Beanie Babies and began selling them for just $5 each.

But Warner didn't just put them on store shelves and hope for the best. He masterminded a launch strategy that would make Beanie Babies one of the biggest toy crazes of the decade.

First, he created scarcity and urgency. Each Beanie Baby was released in a limited quantity, with some designs available for just a few months before being retired. This made them instant collector's items. People couldn't wait to get their hands on the newest releases before they were gone.

Next, Warner built anticipation and buzz. He gave each Beanie Baby a name, birthday, and cute little poem, creating an emotional connection. People started trading, collecting, and chatting about Beanie Babies at swap meets, in online forums, and in line at stores. The buzz was palpable.

Warner was a genius. He turned a simple toy into a must-have item. He did it by expertly using scarcity, urgency, anticipation, and social buzz. At the height of the craze, some rare Beanie Babies sold for thousands of dollars on the secondary market.[13]

The Beanie Babies launch was a masterclass in generating demand. By the late 1990s, the company was making hundreds of millions in sales. And it all started with a simple idea and a brilliant launch strategy.

Why Most Launches Flop (and How to Flip the Script)

You've got a great idea for a course, coaching program, or book. You pour your heart and soul into creating it. Countless late nights, gallons of coffee, and a stiff neck from hunching over your laptop. Finally, after months of hard work, it's ready. You put it out there, expecting a flood of sales and rave reviews. But instead... crickets.

You start to doubt yourself. Was the idea not so great after all? Is your marketing just not cutting it?

Here's the hard truth. Most people create offers without truly validating market demand first. They assume that if they build it, people will come. But that's like cooking a gourmet meal without checking if anyone's even hungry.

Even if your offer is amazing, without the right launch strategy, it can still fall flat. You can't just put it out there and expect people to flock to it. That's where most launches go wrong.

So what's the solution? Two words: Lazy Launch.

Instead of spending months perfecting your offer, you can validate the idea and make sales in just two weeks. Seriously. It's not magic, it's just smart strategy.

The Lazy Launch method is all about building anticipation and urgency. You start by teasing your idea to your audience, getting them curious and excited. Then, you open the cart for a limited time, using scarcity and deadlines to drive sales.

The beauty is you don't even need a finished product. You can presell your idea and use the funds to create the actual offer. This way, you're not wasting time on something no one wants.

It's a bit like a Kickstarter campaign. You're gauging interest and getting people to vote with their wallets before going all-in.

Imagine being able to validate your offer idea in just two weeks with paying customers already lined up. That's the power of a Lazy Launch. It's not about being lazy, it's about being smart with your time and energy.

So if you've been pouring months into offers that aren't selling, it's time to try a different approach. Ditch the crickets and embrace the Lazy Launch. The Lazy Launch is about focusing on the 20% of a normal launch that yields 80% or more of the results. The key is minimal effort with maximum results. Your future self (and your bank account) will thank you.

The Lazy Launch Playbook: Your Step-by-Step Guide to RVP Domination

Okay, so you're sold on the Lazy Launch method. But how do you actually execute it? Here's your step-by-step playbook.

Do a Potential Audience Audit

First up, you need to get a clear picture of your potential reach. And I bet it's wider than you think. List out all your connections across email, social media, online communities, and even your phone contacts. See, we're all more connected than we realize.

Ever heard of the "Six Degrees of Separation" theory? It states that you're connected to any other person on Earth through six or fewer social connections. Wild, right? The point is, when you map out your full network, you'll see that your potential audience is likely much larger than your current followers or email subscribers. We'll teach you how to do this in the next chapter.

Tap Into the 4 Types of Buyers

Next, let's talk psychology. There are four main types of buyers: spontaneous, methodical, social proof, and deadline-driven. If you want to maximize sales, your launch content needs to appeal to each type.

For example, a Visa study found that 82% of consumers research online before making a purchase. Those are your methodical buyers. They need details, FAQs, and clear info about your offer before they'll bite.

On the flip side, your spontaneous buyers respond to excitement and emotion. The lesson? A well-rounded launch includes a mix of content that taps into the main psychological triggers for each buyer type. We'll dive deep into this in chapter fourteen.

Build Anticipation

Now, it's time to start generating some buzz. A week or two before you open registration, start teasing your RVP. Share intriguing snippets about the topic, drop hints about what's coming, and get people curious and excited.

It's like a movie trailer. They're designed to generate maximum anticipation and buzz weeks or even months before the film drops. And there's a reason Hollywood spends millions on trailers - it works. Building anticipation is a critical first step to a successful launch. You want your audience eager and ready to pounce once registration opens.

Create a Buzz

Once anticipation is high, it's time to get people talking. Encourage your audience to comment, share, and post about your upcoming RVP. The more social chatter, the better.

As the saying goes, "Turn your customers into your sales force." When your audience is out there spreading the word, it creates powerful social proof. Seeing other people's excitement makes folks want to be part of the action.

Open Cart with Urgency

When you finally open registration, it's time to crank up the urgency. Set a firm deadline, whether it's a specific date, a time limit, or a cap on spots. Why? Because urgency is one of the most powerful psychological sales triggers out there. I'll teach you how to create anticipation, buzz, and urgency in chapter fifteen.

Think about it like a ticking clock in an action movie. It ratchets up the excitement and forces the hero to act fast. Your launch deadline does the same thing - it motivates people to make a decision now, not later.

Deliver and Exceed Expectations

You've built anticipation, generated buzz, dialed up the urgency, and raked in the sales. Congrats! But now comes the most important part - delivering an RVP that knocks their socks off.

Take a page out of Apple's playbook. They're masters of under-promising and over-delivering. They wow customers with products that exceed expectations. Your goal should be to make your RVP even better than advertised.

See, an outstanding RVP turns one-time buyers into raving fans - the kind that buy from you again and again and tell all their friends. That's how you build a rabid base of repeat customers.

So there you have it - your roadmap to deploy a wildly successful RVP launch. It's not rocket science, but it does take some strategic planning and a little psychological savvy. Master these steps, and you'll be well on your way to launch domination.

In the next few chapters, we will help you implement each step above one section at a time.

Today's Exercise: Brainstorm Your Lazy Launch Ideas

Alright, let's get practical. Grab a pen and paper, set a timer for 15 minutes, and let's brainstorm some killer ideas to inject more anticipation, buzz, and urgency into your RVP launch.

First up, anticipation. How can you get people eagerly waiting for your RVP? Maybe it's a series of teaser emails with intriguing subject lines like "The secret to [desired outcome] is almost here..." or "T-minus 3 days until we unveil the [RVP topic] formula".

Or what about creating a countdown timer on your site? Visuals like that can really ramp up the excitement.

Next, let's generate some buzz. How can you get people talking? One idea is to create shareable graphics with compelling quotes or stats related to your RVP topic. Encourage your audience to share and discuss.

You could also host a pre-launch challenge or contest to engage people and spread the word. For example, "Share your biggest [RVP topic] struggle in the comments for a chance to win a free spot!"

Finally, let's crank up the urgency. What can you do to make people feel like they can't miss out? Limited-time bonuses work great. Maybe it's a 1-on-1 strategy call, a bonus resource pack, or an exclusive community invite for the first 20 registrants.

Or you could create some scarcity by limiting the number of spots available. "Only 30 seats remaining for [RVP name]! Lock in your spot before we sell out!"

The key is to get creative and specific. Don't just say, "doors are closing soon." Give concrete deadlines like "Registration closes at midnight EST this Friday!"

Okay, time's up! Look at your list. Pick the 3-5 strongest ideas and weave them into your launch plan. The more you can amp up anticipation, buzz, and urgency, the more irresistible your RVP will be.

Remember, a little psychology can go a long way in boosting your launch results. So, don't be afraid to tap into those powerful mental triggers.

Your audience will be so fired up that they'll be scrambling to smash that "buy now" button when your RVP drops. And that's exactly what we want, right?

So, take action on this exercise. It's not just theory, it's your launch success blueprint. Let's make it happen!

Key Takeaways:

- A simple 2-week launch plan lets you validate demand and make sales fast before creating your full offer. This is the power of the Rapid Validation Product approach.

- Successful launches build anticipation and buzz in the first week, then use urgency psychology to drive registrations in week two when the "cart opens."

- Deliver an exceptional RVP to turn buyers into repeat customers and raving fans. The first sale is just the beginning of the relationship.

13

Create Your Potential Audience Audit

B efore J.K. Rowling became a household name, before Harry Potter took the world by storm, she was just another aspiring writer with a dream. Tucked away in a small Edinburgh flat, Rowling poured her heart into the story of a young wizard, not knowing if anyone would ever read it.

Like many writers, Rowling felt isolated and uncertain. She had no publishing connections. She had no huge social media following (this was the early 90s, after all). And, she had no way of knowing if her work would resonate with readers. In short, she felt like she had no audience.

But Rowling did have something: a small but mighty network of friends, family, and former colleagues. People who knew her believed in her and were willing to support her journey.

When Rowling finished her first Harry Potter manuscript, she didn't have a huge platform from which to launch. But she did have a few close connections. She reached out to an old friend from her days working at Amnesty International, who put her in touch with a literary agent. That agent saw the magic in Rowling's words and agreed to represent her.

The rest, as they say, is history. Harry Potter and the Philosopher's Stone was published in 1997. It launched a global phenomenon.

The series spans seven books, eight films, theme parks, and much merchandise.

But it all started with Rowling recognizing the potential in her existing network. She didn't have a massive audience at the start, but she had something just as powerful: a small group of people who were ready to champion her work.[14]

This chapter is all about uncovering that hidden potential in your own network. We'll cover a process called the Potential Audience Audit. It will help you see how many people you could reach by using your existing connections.

Here's the thing: you don't need a massive following to validate your offer and make sales. You just need to start with the people who are already in your corner. As Rowling's story shows, even the most successful journeys can start with a single connection.

So if you're feeling like you don't have an audience, take heart. Your potential reach is probably much greater than you realize. Let's uncover it together.

The Audience Myth: Why You Don't Need a Huge Following to Launch

Let's talk about a common belief that holds many people back from launching their offer: the idea that you need a massive audience to be successful.

Here's what most people do. They look at their social media following, see a modest number (or even a big fat zero), and think, "I can't possibly launch yet. I need thousands of followers first!" So they put their offer on hold, waiting for that elusive "big break" that will magically bring in a huge audience.

But here's the problem with that approach. By waiting for a huge following, you're missing out on the potential audience that's already right in front of you.

You see, most people have a much larger network than they realize. You likely have access to many potential customers. They are in your social media contacts, your email list, your friends, your family, and your colleagues.

But when you're stuck in the "I need a huge audience" mindset, you overlook those valuable connections. You miss out on opportunities to validate your offer, get feedback, and even make sales.

So what's the alternative? It's time to conduct a Potential Audience Audit.

Untapped Potential: How to Discover Your Hidden Audience

A Potential Audience Audit is all about uncovering the hidden reach of your existing network. It's a process of mapping all the people you're connected to, directly or indirectly. It's about getting a clear picture of your true audience potential.

This audit involves a few key steps. First, you list out all your social media accounts and note your follower count on each. Then, you export your email contacts from all your accounts. Next, you identify your "Top 50" - the 50 people you have the strongest, most engaged relationships with.

By the end of this audit, you'll have a clear, data-backed picture of your potential reach. And spoiler alert: it's probably much higher than you think.

The Power of Connection: Leveraging Your Network for Launch Success

Once you've done your Potential Audience Audit, it's time to put that insight into action.

This is where the magic happens. Instead of waiting for a huge, anonymous audience, you start engaging with the people already in your network. You let them know about your upcoming offer. You ask for their feedback and support.

Remember, these are people who already know you, like you, and want to see you succeed. They're much more likely to engage with your offer than cold leads who don't have that personal connection.

And as you start to validate your offer with your existing network, something amazing happens. Those initial supporters start spreading the word. They share your offer with their networks. Momentum builds. And before you know it, your audience starts to grow organically.

That's the power of starting with the audience you already have rather than waiting for the audience you wish you had.

So don't let the "I need a huge following" myth hold you back. Your audience is already there, waiting to be uncovered. All you need is a Potential Audience Audit and the courage to start connecting.

How to Conduct Your Potential Audience Audit

Alright, let's break down the steps to create your Potential Audience Audit. Grab a pen and paper, or fire up a spreadsheet, and let's get started.

Step 1. List Your Social Media Accounts

First up, make a list of all your active social media accounts. Facebook, Instagram, Twitter, LinkedIn - write 'em all down. Then, next to each one, note how many followers or friends you have on that platform.

Now, I know what you might be thinking. "But my follower count is so small!" Here's the thing, though. Even if you only have 100 followers on Instagram, that's still 100 potential customers. And when you consider the "Six Degrees of Separation" theory, it suggests that everyone is connected by no more than six social links. Your reach could be larger than you think.

Takeaway: Don't underestimate the power of your social media audience, no matter the size. Those connections can be the start of something big.

Step 2: Export Your Email Contacts

Next, it's time to round up your email contacts. Log into all your email accounts. These include your personal, work, and that old Hotmail address you still use for some reason. Then, export your contacts into a CSV file or spreadsheet.

If you're thinking, "Do I really need to include all my accounts?", the answer is yes. A study by The Radicati Group found that the average person has 1.75 email accounts. That means you likely have contacts scattered across multiple inboxes, and each one is a potential lead.

Takeaway: Your email contacts are a gold mine of potential audience members. Don't leave any stone unturned in your audit.

Step 3: Identify Your Top 50 Connections

Now, out of all your social media followers and email contacts, who are the 50 people you have the strongest relationships with? They could be close friends, family members, colleagues, or just acquaintances. You've had great conversations with them.

Write down their names. These are your "Top 50". As Porter Gale says, "Your network is your net worth." These 50 people are your inner circle, your champions. They're the ones most likely to support your launch, give you honest feedback, and spread the word about your offer.

Takeaway: Your Top 50 are your secret weapon. Nurture those relationships, and they'll be the foundation of your launch success.

Step 4: Estimate Your Potential Audience Reach

Finally, it's time to crunch some numbers. Using industry-standard reach estimates, calculate the potential audience you could tap into through your social media followers, email contacts, and Top 50.

For example, if you have 1,000 Instagram followers. The average user has 150 followers. So, your potential reach on Instagram could be 150,000 people (1,000 x 150 = 150,000).

It's like an iceberg. Your immediate following is just the tip - there's a whole lot more beneath the surface. Or think of it like a tree. Your direct connections are the branches. But, they lead to a vast network of roots. These are the roots of your connections and their connections.

Your Potential Audience Audit will likely reveal a larger audience than you thought at first. That's the reach you have to work with as you validate and launch your offer.

Remember, this audit isn't about collecting a huge, faceless crowd. It's about seeing the value in your current connections. You can use those relationships to build momentum.

So don't get discouraged by small numbers. In the world of launching, your network is your superpower. Audit it, nurture it, and watch it grow.

Today's Exercise: Conduct Your Potential Audience Audit

Alright, it's time to put all this theory into practice. Let's dive into your Potential Audience Audit.

Here's what I want you to do. Set a timer for 15 minutes, and commit to focusing solely on this exercise for that time. No distractions, no excuses. This is important work.

First, open up a new document or grab a fresh piece of paper. Start by listing out all your active social media accounts. Facebook, Twitter, Instagram, LinkedIn, TikTok - if you've got a profile, write it down.

Next to each account, note down your current follower or friend count. Don't worry if the numbers seem small. Remember, we're looking at the potential here, not just hard numbers.

Next, hop over to your email accounts. Yes, all of them. Export your contacts from each account into a CSV file or spreadsheet. If you're not sure how to do this, a quick Google search will give you step-by-step instructions for your specific email provider.

Once you've got all your email contacts in one place, it's time to identify your Top 50. These are the 50 people you have the strongest, most positive relationships with. They could be friends, family, colleagues, mentors - anyone you feel would be supportive of your launch.

Write down their names. If you're feeling extra motivated, jot down a few notes about each person. How do you know them? When was the last time you connected?

Finally, it's time to estimate your total potential reach. This is where a little math comes in handy.

For each social media account, multiply your follower count by 100. Why 100? It's a conservative estimate of how many people each of your followers could potentially reach.

So, if you have 500 Instagram followers, your potential Instagram reach is 50,000 (500 x 100 = 50,000).

Do this for each social media account and add up the totals. Then, add the number of email contacts you exported. Finally, add 50 (for your Top 50).

The grand total? That's your estimated potential audience reach.

I bet it's a bigger number than you expected. That's the power of the Potential Audience Audit - it reveals the hidden reach of your existing network.

But this exercise isn't just about numbers. It's about strategy. Now that you know your potential reach, it's time to make a plan to tap into it.

As you look at your Top 50 list, start thinking about how you could reach out to each person when you're ready to validate your offer.

Could you send a personal email? Schedule a coffee chat. Invite them to a special preview of your offer.

The key is to make it personal. These are your champions, your inner circle. Treat them as such.

As for your wider network - your social media followers and email contacts - start brainstorming ways to warm them up to your upcoming offer. Could you share teaser posts about the problem your offer solves? Could you run a survey to gauge their interest and pain points?

The Potential Audience Audit isn't just a one-and-done exercise. It's a living, breathing strategy document. Keep it handy as you move through the validation and launch process.

Remember, your network is your most valuable asset as you launch. This audit is your roadmap to leveraging it effectively.

So don't skimp on this exercise. Put in the time, put in the thought, and watch as your perception of your audience potential shifts.

You've got this. Your audience is out there, waiting for what you have to offer. It's time to start connecting with them.

Key Takeaways:

- Your audience could be much larger than your followers. It includes your social media contacts, email contacts, and friends.

- Conducting a Potential Audience Audit is a key step. It helps find your hidden audience before you validate and launch your offer.

- By leveraging your existing network, you can reach a wider audience, validate your offer, and make sales, even without a large following.

14
Understanding the 4 Types of Buyers

D avid Ogilvy knew how to sell to people. His famous ad campaign for Rolls-Royce in the 1960s proved it. The headline read, "At 60 miles an hour the loudest noise in this new Rolls-Royce comes from the electric clock." Ogilvy understood that different people buy for different reasons. Some are spontaneous, jumping at the chance to own the latest and greatest. Others are methodical, needing every last detail before making a move. Then there are the social-proof buyers who look at what others are doing. And, of course, the deadline-driven folks who wait until the last minute to decide.

Ogilvy's Rolls-Royce ad had something for everyone. The spontaneous buyers were hooked by the novelty of an electric clock being the loudest noise in a car. The methodical crowd got their fill. They heard about technical details. They learned about the vehicle's construction and performance. Social proof came from the implication that Rolls-Royce cars were the choice of discerning buyers. And the deadline-driven? Well, they knew they had to act fast if they wanted to be seen driving the latest status symbol.

The results spoke for themselves. The ad campaign was a smashing success, cementing Rolls-Royce's reputation as the ultimate luxury car. And it was all because David Ogilvy understood the four types of buyers and how to appeal to each of them.[15]

So, what does this have to do with you and your validation offers? Everything. If you want to turn your ideas into income, you need to know how to sell to all four buyer types. In this chapter, we'll dive deep into what makes each type tick and how you can craft your messaging to resonate with them. Get ready to take your offers from "meh" to "must-have."

Understanding the 4 Types of Buyers

You've poured your heart and soul into creating an offer that you know will change lives. You've spent countless hours perfecting every detail, from the content to the packaging. You hit publish, sit back, and wait for the sales to roll in. But crickets. Nada. Zilch.

What gives? Chances are, you've fallen into the trap that snags so many entrepreneurs. You're using a one-size-fits-all approach to marketing, trying to sell to everyone the same way. But here's the thing: we all buy differently. Some of us are impulsive, ready to whip out our wallets at the first sign of something shiny and new. Others need to mull it over, do their research, and weigh every pro and con before making a move.

You fail to account for these buyer motivations and decision-making processes. Then, you're leaving money on the table. A lot of it. You might as well be shouting into the void, hoping that someone, anyone, will hear you and take action.

But it doesn't have to be this way. The secret to selling successfully? Segmentation. Divide your audience into four buyer types. Tailor your messaging to each group. This way, you can create marketing that resonates deeply. No more wasted ad spend or lackluster launches.

Think about it like this. If you were selling a car, would you use the same pitch for a speed demon who craves new things as for a cautious family man who puts safety first? Of course not. So why would you use the same approach for your offers?

Next, we'll cover the four buyer types. We'll see how to craft your marketing to appeal to each group's unique mind and journey. Get ready to watch your sales soar.

4 Types of Buyers

Ready to rev up your sales engine? Here are the four steps to mastering the art of selling to all buyer types:

Type 1. Spontaneous Buyers

First up, let's talk about those spontaneous buyers. They're the ones who get fired up about anything new and exciting. To hook them, you need to emphasize novelty and spark their curiosity. Think about those impulse purchases at the supermarket checkout. Spontaneous buyers just can't resist something fresh and intriguing. Your key takeaway? Play up the newness factor to get these folks on board.

Type 2. Methodical Buyers

Next, we've got the methodical buyers. These are the people who carefully weigh every decision and need all the details before taking the plunge. They're not going to buy on a whim - they want to know exactly what they're getting into. Research shows that providing comprehensive product info can boost conversions by a whopping 80%. So, your mission is to preemptively address any questions or concerns these meticulous buyers might have.

Type 3. Social Proof Buyers

Now, let's talk about the social proof buyers. They're the ones who look to others' experiences to validate their own purchase decisions. They want to know that they're making a smart choice, and they trust the opinions of people who have been there and done that. As psychologist Robert Cialdini put it, "We view a behavior as more correct in a given situation to the degree that we see others performing it." Your key takeaway? Leverage customer success stories and testimonials to show these buyers that they're in good company.

Type 4. Deadline-Driven Buyers

Finally, we've got the deadline-driven buyers. These folks are motivated by scarcity and limited-time opportunities. They don't want to miss out on a good thing, so they'll wait until the last minute to make their move. Just look at the California Gold Rush of 1849 - hordes of buyers were clamoring to stake their claims before it was too late. Your key takeaway? Use time-sensitive offers and highlight the fear of missing out to light a fire under these buyers and compel them to act.

Master these four types of buyers, and you'll be well on your way to selling to all buyer types like a pro. In the next section, we'll dive into some practical exercises you can use to put this knowledge into action.

Today's Exercise: Find an Idea for Each Buyer Type

Alright, let's get practical. It's time to put all this buyer-type knowledge to work and start crafting some killer marketing messages.

Here's your mission, should you choose to accept it: block off 10-15 minutes right now and dive into a brainstorming session. Your goal? To come up with ways to incorporate appeals to each buyer type in your validation offer messaging.

Start by thinking about your offer from the perspective of each buyer type. What would hook a spontaneous buyer? How can you provide the details that methodical buyers crave? What social proof can you leverage to win over skeptics? And how can you create a sense of urgency for those deadline-driven folks?

Jot down every idea that comes to mind, no matter how wild or out-there it might seem. Remember, this is brainstorming - there are no wrong answers.

Once you've got a solid list of ideas, it's time to start crafting your messages. Take one idea for each buyer type and flesh it out into a full-fledged marketing message. Think about the language, tone, and style that will resonate with each group.

For example, your message for spontaneous buyers might be: "Introducing the brand-new XYZ program. It's the freshest, most exciting way to [achieve desired result]. Get in on the ground floor before everyone else catches on!"

For methodical buyers, you might say: "Discover the proven XYZ system for [achieving desired result]. Our program includes many details about what's included. So, you know exactly what you're getting. Plus, our 30-day money-back guarantee means you can try it risk-free."

Your social proof message could be: "Join the thousands of [target audience]. They have already achieved [desired result] with the XYZ program. Here's what just a few of them have to say: [insert testimonials]."

For buyers with deadlines, you might say: "Last chance to get the XYZ program for $X! This offer ends in [timeframe], so grab this chance to [achieve desired result]."

Crafting these targeted messages will help you connect with each buyer type more deeply. It will also increase the likelihood of them saying "yes" to your offer. Give it a try and see how it impacts your sales.

Key Takeaways:

- Cater to all four buyer types. They are: spontaneous, methodical, social proof, and deadline-driven. This will help you sell your validation offers like hotcakes.

- Match your marketing to each group's unique motivations and watch your sales soar.

- Sprinkle in novelty, information, social proof, and urgency to make your offer irresistible to every buyer type.

15

The 3 Secrets to Selling Anything

Y ou're scrolling through your Twitter feed (before it became known as X), and it's August 2019. Suddenly, you see a tweet from Popeyes. It's an image of their new chicken sandwich. It has a subtle jab at their rival, Chick-fil-A. But they didn't know this tweet would start an unprecedented fast-food frenzy.

Within days, the Popeyes chicken sandwich was the talk of the internet. Social media was flooded with reviews, memes, and debates. People were lining up for hours just to get a taste. The buzz was so intense that Popeyes locations started running out of the sandwich.

But here's the genius part: instead of rushing to restock, Popeyes let the anticipation build. They made a public announcement that the sandwich would be back soon. People were marking their calendars, setting reminders, telling their friends. The urgency was palpable - when that sandwich returned, you had to be first in line.

And boy, did that strategy pay off. When the sandwich made its triumphant return in November, people waited in lines that wrapped around city blocks. Drive-thru lanes caused traffic jams. Popeyes sold as many chicken sandwiches in two weeks as they had projected to sell through the end of September.

The Popeyes chicken sandwich craze is a masterclass in selling anything. It shows the three secrets: anticipation, buzz, and urgency. They teased the product, let the public anticipation and social media buzz reach a fever pitch, and then created a sense of "now or never" urgency.[16]

This chapter is all about harnessing those same three secrets for your own offer. Whether you're selling a physical product, a digital course, or a service, the principles are the same. Build anticipation, generate buzz, and create urgency, and you'll have customers lining up virtual blocks to buy from you.

Now, you might be thinking, "That's great for a big brand like Popeyes, but how does this apply to my small business?" The truth is, these secrets work no matter your size or industry. They can be even more powerful for small businesses and personal brands. This is because you have the agility and personal touch that big corporations can only dream of.

In this chapter, we're going to dive into exactly how to implement anticipation, buzz, and urgency in your next offer launch. I'll show you how to use a simple two-week "lazy launch" plan. It will test your offer idea and get your first sales. It will also appeal to the four main types of buyers.

Here's the thing: when you master these three secrets, you're not just creating a successful launch. You're building a loyal fan base of customers who are eager to buy from you again and again. You're setting yourself up for long-term, sustainable success.

So get ready to take some notes because we're about to unlock the psychology of selling. By the end of this chapter, you'll have a proven plan for turning your offer idea into a sold-out success. Let's dive in.

The Missing Ingredients: Why Most Product Launches Fall Flat

Let's talk about the typical approach to launching a product or service. Most people pour their heart and soul into creating something amazing. They spend weeks, months, maybe even years perfecting their offer. And then, when it's finally ready, they put it out into the world and wait.

They post about it on social media, maybe send an email to their list, and then hope that the sales will start rolling in. But more often than not, they're met with crickets. A few nibbles here and there, but nothing like the flood of sales they were hoping for.

So what's going wrong? Why aren't people flocking to buy this incredible thing you've created?

The problem is that most people lack three key ingredients for a successful launch: anticipation, buzz, and urgency. They're relying on the inherent value of their product or service to sell itself. But the truth is, even the best offer can fall flat without the right launch strategy.

Think about it. When was the last time you bought something just because it existed? Chances are, there was something that got you excited about it first. Maybe you saw a friend raving about it on Facebook. Maybe there was a limited-time discount that made you feel like you had to act fast. Maybe the brand had been teasing the launch for weeks, and you couldn't wait to get your hands on it.

That's the power of anticipation, buzz, and urgency. They're the psychological triggers that turn passive browsing into active buying.

And without them, your launch is like a car without an engine - it might look nice, but it's not going anywhere.

So what's the solution? How can you ensure your next launch has that crucial momentum?

The Two-Week Lazy Launch Method

Enter the two-week "lazy launch". The framework is simple but very effective. It builds anticipation, generates buzz, and creates urgency. It also validates your offer idea and appeals to the four main types of buyers.

Here's how it works: in the first week, you focus on creating anticipation. This is all about teasing your upcoming offer, giving sneak peeks, and hinting at something exciting to come. You might do a survey to gauge interest, share behind-the-scenes content, or start a countdown. The goal is to get your audience curious and eager to learn more.

Then, in the second week, you open the doors to your offer. But you don't just slap a "buy now" button on your website and call it a day. Instead, you actively generate buzz and urgency. You might host a webinar, run a challenge, or offer a limited-time bonus. You encourage your buyers to share their excitement on social media. And you make it clear that this opportunity won't last forever - there's a deadline, and if they don't act now, they might miss out.

By structuring your launch in this way, you're not just telling people about your offer - you're taking them on a psychological journey. You're building excitement, fostering a sense of community and social proof, and motivating them to take action.

And the best part? This approach works for any kind of offer, whether you're selling a physical product, a digital course, a service, or even hosting a paid workshop. The principles are universal.

So if you've been struggling to get traction with your launches, it's time to ditch the "hope and pray" method. Instead, embrace the power of anticipation, buzz, and urgency. In the rest of this chapter, I'll show you exactly how to implement this two-week lazy launch framework, step by step.

Get ready to transform the way you launch forever. Your offer deserves to be seen, celebrated and sold out. Let's make it happen.

Alright, let's dive into the nitty-gritty of how to actually implement the three secrets to selling anything in your next launch. We'll break it down into three key steps: creating anticipation, generating buzz, and injecting urgency.

Secret 1: Create Anticipation (Week 1)

The first step is all about building anticipation in the week leading up to your launch. This is your chance to get your audience excited and curious about what's to come.

One of the most effective ways to do this is to survey your audience. Ask them about their pain points, their desires, and what they'd love to see in your upcoming offer. This not only gives you valuable insights for crafting your offer, but it also makes your audience feel heard and involved. They'll be eager to see how you've incorporated their feedback.

Another key tactic is to tease your offer. Share sneak peeks, behind-the-scenes glimpses, or cryptic hints about what's to come. You want to give just enough information to pique their interest, but not so much that there's no mystery left.

Think of it like a movie trailer. A good trailer gives you a tantalizing glimpse of the story, the characters, and the action, but it doesn't give away the entire plot. It leaves you wanting more, counting down the days until the movie's release. That's the same feeling you want to create in your audience.

Here's a simple template you can use:

- Day 1. Float the idea (I'm thinking about hosting a workshop on Zoom about [Workshop Topic]. Interested?)

- Day 3. Survey (What are your biggest challenges when it comes to [Workshop Topic]?

- Day 5. I'm doing it! (Looks like you guys want to know more about this so I'm doing it! be on the lookout next week for more details)

The goal in this first week is to grab the attention of those spontaneous buyers - the ones who are always drawn to what's new and exciting. By building anticipation, you're using their love of new things. You're making your offer feel like a can't-miss event.

Secret 2: Generate Buzz (Week 2 - Part 1)

Once you've built that initial anticipation, it's time to open the doors to your offer and start generating some serious buzz. This is where you get people talking, sharing, and engaging with your launch.

One powerful way to do this is to encourage social sharing. Create shareable graphics, write compelling social media posts, and directly ask your audience to spread the word. You could even run a contest or giveaway for people who share your launch on social media.

Another tactic is to leverage influencers or affiliates. Reach out to people with audiences similar to yours and ask them to promote your offer. This can quickly expand your reach and add credibility to your launch

The key here is to generate those high-arousal emotions - excitement, enthusiasm, and even a little FOMO (fear of missing out). A study by Jonah Berger found that these types of emotions can increase social sharing by up to 34%. When people are excited about something, they naturally want to talk about it and share it with others.

Here's a simple timeline you can use:

- Day 8. Spontaneous Buyers – Okay, you can now register for the workshop! (Tip. On social media, DM everyone who said they were interested the link to join your workshop)

- Day 9. Methodical Buyers – Send a FAQ email answering all the questions people might have (Tip. Post the same info on social media too!)

- Day 10. Social Proof Buyers – Share a comment from someone who is excited about your offer or share how many spots you have left

- Day 12-14. Deadline-Driven Buyers – Send a few emails (and social posts) the last two days before you close the offer (Tip. It's common for 25-50% of your sales to come in the last 24 hours so keep pushing!)

This buzz phase is crucial for appealing to the methodical researchers and the social proof seekers in your audience. The researchers will comb through all the chatter and information about your offer. They'll look for signs that it's a good investment. The social proof seekers will be watching. They want to see who else is getting excited about your launch. They want to be part of something that's popular and talked-about.

Secret 3: Inject Urgency (Week 2 - Part 2)

In the final days of your launch, it's time to ramp up the urgency. This is where you push those on-the-fence prospects to make a decision by reminding them that the opportunity won't last forever.

The most obvious tactic here is to set a firm deadline. Make it clear that the cart is closing, the bonuses are going away, or the price is going up at a specific date and time. Use a countdown timer on your sales page to visually reinforce that ticking clock.

Another way to create urgency is to communicate scarcity. Highlight the limited number of spots available, the finite supply of a physical product, or the exclusive nature of your bonuses. When people feel like they might miss out on something special, they're more motivated to take action.

It's also powerful to emphasize the cost of inaction. Remind your audience what they stand to lose if they don't take advantage of your offer. Will they continue to struggle with the problem your product solves? Will they miss out on a unique opportunity to learn and grow? Make them feel the pain of passing up your offer.

As Jim Rohn famously said, "Without a sense of urgency, desire loses its value." Urgency gives your offer an expiration date, a reason to act now instead of later.

This is the key to converting those deadline-driven buyers. These are the people who always wait until the last minute, who need that extra push to finally make a decision. By injecting urgency into your launch, you're giving them the motivation they need to commit.

Remember, your job isn't over once you've made the sale. The final step is to deliver on your promises and wow your new customers. But by using anticipation, buzz, and urgency in your launch, you set yourself up for success. You appeal to all four buyer types and make your offer feel truly irresistible.

Today's Exercise: Mapping Out Your Lazy Launch Plan

Alright, it's time to put these secrets into action. Grab a pen and paper, set a timer for 15 minutes, and let's brainstorm some concrete ways you can create anticipation, buzz, and urgency in your next launch.

First, let's think about anticipation. How can you get your audience excited and curious before your launch even begins? Here are a few ideas to get you started:

- Share sneak peeks: Give your followers a behind-the-scenes look at your process, your product, or your planning. Show them just enough to pique their interest but not so much that there's no surprise left.

- Run a countdown: Start a countdown to your launch date on social media. You could post daily teasers, clues, or mini-challenges to keep people engaged and excited.

- Tease a big revelation. Hint that you'll make a big announcement. You'll reveal something game-changing in your up-coming launch. Build that sense of "I wonder what it could be?".

Next, let's brainstorm some ideas for generating buzz once your launch is underway:

- Host a viral challenge: Create a challenge related to your offer that people can participate in and share on social media. Make it fun, engaging, and visually shareable.

- Leverage influencers: Reach out to influencers or thought leaders in your niche and ask them to share your offer with their audience. A shout-out from a respected figure can lend instant credibility and buzz to your launch.

- Encourage user-generated content. Ask your buyers and followers to share their experience with your offer on social media. You could create a branded hashtag, run a contest for the best post, or feature user content on your own channels.

Finally, let's think about how to inject some urgency into your launch:

- Offer a fast-action bonus: Give a special bonus or discount to the first X number of buyers. This creates a sense of competition and motivates people to act fast.

- Use a countdown timer: Place a visible countdown timer on your sales page, ticking down to the moment your offer closes or your price goes up. This visual cue is a powerful psychological trigger.

- Emphasize scarcity: Highlight the limited nature of your offer. Is it only available to a certain number of people? Is it a one-time opportunity? Make it clear that this chance won't come again.

Now, look at your list of ideas. Which ones feel most exciting to you? Which ones align best with your offer and your audience? Pick your top strategies for anticipation, buzz, and urgency, and start making a plan to implement them in your next launch.

Remember, the goal isn't to use all of these tactics at once - that could feel overwhelming for both you and your audience. Instead, choose the ones that feel most authentic and impactful and focus on executing them well.

The beauty of this brainstorming exercise is that it gets your creative juices flowing. You might come up with ideas that are totally unique to your business and your offer. Trust those instincts - often, the most effective launch strategies are the ones that feel fresh and original.

So take this list and run with it. Tweak these ideas to fit your style, your offer, and your audience. The more you can infuse your own personality and flair into your launch, the more engaging and memorable it will be.

And as you implement these strategies, pay attention to what works. Notice which tactics generate the most excitement, the most shares, and the most sales. Over time, you'll develop a fine-tuned sense of what resonates with your specific audience.

Creating anticipation, buzz, and urgency is part art, part science. But with this brainstorming exercise, you're well on your way to mastering both.

Key Takeaways:

- The three secrets to selling anything are anticipation, buzz, and urgency. When used together, they can dramatically boost sales and appeal to all four types of buyers.

- Anticipation is about building excitement and curiosity before the launch. Buzz is about getting people talking and sharing during the launch. Urgency is about motivating immediate action before the deadline.

- Implementing the three secrets doesn't have to be complicated. A simple two-week "lazy launch" can be highly effective in validating your offer and generating sales.

16

The Power of Offer Stacking

"Would you like fries with that?" You've probably heard this famous phrase countless times at McDonald's. But did you know it's actually a brilliant marketing strategy called cross-selling?

Cross-selling is about offering related products. They complement what your customer is already buying. And McDonald's has absolutely nailed it. Think about it - you've already committed to that juicy burger, so why not add some crispy fries to complete the meal? It just makes sense.[17]

And that's exactly what offer stacking is all about. By providing a range of products at different price points that build on each other, you can massively boost your sales and revenue. Just as fries elevate a humble burger, offer stacking lifts your business. It gives customers an irresistible value ladder to climb.

In this chapter, we'll dive deep into the psychology behind why offer stacking works so well. You'll learn how to craft the perfect combo of entry-level, core, and high-end offerings that'll have your customers hungry for more. Plus, we'll explore the power of recurring revenue products to keep 'em coming back like loyal McDonald's regulars.

So buckle up and get ready to supersize your sales with the magic of offer stacking!

The Power of Offer Stacking

You've poured your heart and soul into creating an incredible offer. Your course or coaching program is packed with value, and you know it can transform lives. But here's the thing: if you're only putting out one offer, you're leaving a ton of money on the table.

It's a common mistake that so many coaches and course creators make. They think that one killer offer is enough to maximize sales and revenue. But the truth is, a chunk of your audience will always be hungry for more. They're ready and willing to invest even further in their success - if you give them the chance.

Picture this: you've just wrapped up an amazing paid workshop, and your attendees are buzzing with excitement. They're fired up and ready to take action. But then what? If you lack a next-step offer, you're missing a golden chance. It can deepen that relationship and help them get even better results.

Imagine saying something like, "You now have the knowledge to crush it with this strategy. But how would you like to actually implement it together, with my guidance every step of the way? I'm inviting a small group of dedicated folks to join me for a transformative 4-week group coaching experience. Who's in?"

Boom. You've just opened the door to a whole new level of impact and income. And the best part? You're not starting from scratch. You're adding to the foundation you've laid. You're giving your best customers a chance to reach new heights.

But here's the key: it's not just about having any old upsell. It's about crafting a range of offers that meet your customers where they are and guide them toward their ultimate goals. It's about stacking your offerings like a ladder, with each rung leading to the next level of transformation.

Think about it this way: some people might be total newbies, just dipping their toes into your world. They might not be ready to dive headfirst into your high-end mastermind or one-on-one coaching. But they'd be thrilled to snag a bite-sized course or workshop that gives them a taste of what's possible.

On the flip side, you've got your die-hard fans who are all in. They've devoured everything you've put out there, and they're hungry for more. They're ready to invest serious time and money into achieving massive results. And if you don't have a premium offer that meets them at that level, you're doing them (and yourself) a disservice.

The beauty of offer stacking is that it allows you to serve your entire audience, no matter where they are in their journey. You are not just serving one market. You are making a custom path to success for all who resonate with your message.

So don't settle for a one-hit wonder. Create a symphony of offers that build upon each other, and watch as your impact (and your income) soar to new heights.

How to Create Your Offer Stack

Alright, let's dive into the nitty-gritty of how to actually implement offer stacking in your business. It's not as complicated as you might think, but it does require a bit of strategic planning.

Step 1. Start with Your Core Offer

This is the foundation of your offer stack, the meaty main course that everything else is built around. For most coaches and course creators, this is one of the four validation offers we talked about earlier. They are a low-content book, a 1-day virtual workshop, a mini-course, or a 4-week group coaching program.

Think of this core offer as a sneak peek into your genius. It's a chance for potential customers to get a taste of what you're all about without having to commit to a huge investment right off the bat.

And here's a fun fact: In 2012, a study in the Journal of Consumer Research found that by offering a low-priced option, businesses could boost sales at all price points. Crazy, right?

The takeaway? Don't underestimate the power of an entry-level offer. It's the perfect way to attract new customers and prime them for your higher-priced products down the line.

Step 2. Develop a Next Step Upsell Offer

Now that you've got your core offer in place, it's time to kick things up a notch. Here, you'll create a high-octane, premium offering. It promises mind-blowing results for your top customers.

We're talking about offerings like a four-week boot camp, a more in-depth mini-course, or an intensive one-day workshop. These kinds of offerings will have your customers salivating at the chance to work with you on a deeper level.

Take Gary Halbert, for example. When this legendary copywriter launched his newsletter, he didn't just stop there. He offered a premium $3000 personal coaching upsell that became a major cash cow for his business.

The lesson? Don't be scared to go big with your premium offerings. Your most dedicated customers will jump at the chance to invest heavily in something that promises extraordinary results.

Step 3. Integrate Your Offers into a Seamless Customer Journey

Here's where the magic really happens. It's not enough to just have a bunch of awesome offers floating around - you've got to make sure they fit together like a perfect puzzle.

Picture your offer stack like a set of Russian nesting dolls. Each offer should build on the last one. They should guide your customer to their ultimate transformation smoothly and naturally.

Take some time to map out exactly how your offerings connect with each other. How does your entry-level product lead into your core offer? How does your core offer set the stage for your premium upsell? It's all about crafting a cohesive journey that feels effortless for your customer.

When you nail this step, you're not just maximizing your revenue. You're making an unforgettable customer experience that'll keep folks coming back.

Bonus. Introduce a Recurring Revenue Offer

Want to know the secret sauce to a wildly profitable business? Two words: recurring revenue.

By making a subscription product, like a membership site or group coaching program, you give yourself the gift of steady income month after month.

As membership site expert Stu McLaren puts it, "Recurring revenue is the holy grail for entrepreneurs. It provides the stability and predictability to really scale."

A recurring offer adds the stability needed to your bottom line. It also lets you serve your customers better over time. It's a win-win!

So there you have it - the step-by-step breakdown of how to implement offer stacking in your business. It might take a bit of elbow grease to get all the pieces in place, but trust me, it's so worth it. With the right offer stack, you'll be able to serve your customers at the highest level while also exploding your revenue like never before.

Today's Exercise: Choose an Offer Stack

Alright, it's time to roll up your sleeves and put this offer stacking stuff into action! I know it might feel a little overwhelming at first, but trust me, once you get the hang of it, it's like riding a bike. A really profitable, customer-delighting bike.

So here's your mission, should you choose to accept it: take the next 10-15 minutes to brainstorm some ideas for an offer stack that you can attach to your core validation offer.

Now, I know what you might be thinking. "But Jonathan, I'm already putting so much effort into my main offer. How the am I supposed to come up with even more stuff?" Well, fear not, my friend. I've got a few ideas to get those creative juices flowing.

Let's say your core validation offer is a virtual workshop. You've poured your heart and soul into creating an incredible live training that delivers massive value. Awesome! But what if you could take that experience even further? Enter the 4-week bootcamp upsell. Imagine giving your students the chance to dive deeper. They can do so with weekly live calls, personalized feedback, and a tight-knit community of like-minded folks. It's like the ultimate VIP experience!

Or maybe your core offer is a low-content book - a bite-sized intro to your amazing expertise. Why not follow that up with a more comprehensive mini-course that builds on those foundational concepts? You could package it up with some video lessons, worksheets, and a private Facebook group for added support. Talk about taking things to the next level!

And if you're running a 4-week group coaching program as your main offer, why not let your students continue the magic with some ongoing 1-on-1 coaching? You could offer a discounted rate for a 3-month package or even create a premium tier with unlimited email access and monthly strategy calls. The possibilities are endless!

The key here is to think about how these different offers can work together to create an incredible customer journey. You don't just slap together random products. You craft a seamless experience. It guides your people to their ultimate change.

So, take a few minutes to jot down some ideas. Don't worry about getting it perfect - just let your imagination run wild. Picture your dream customer and think about what kind of offer stack would absolutely blow their mind. What kind of results could you help them achieve? What kind of support would make them feel like the most valued customer in the world?

Remember, the beauty of offer stacking is that it allows you to serve your people at the highest level while also creating a seriously lucrative business. It's a win-win-win all around!

So go ahead, grab a notebook, open up a fresh document, and start brainstorming. I can't wait to see what you come up with.

Key Takeaways:

- Offer stacking lets you serve customers at every stage of their journey and price sensitivity. It covers entry-level to high-end.

- A percentage of your audience will buy more from you if you make it available to them.

- Integrating your stack into a clear ascension path is key. It helps you maximize sales and deliver a great customer experience.

17

Pillar 4. Debrief (Your Key Validation Metrics)

Two young entrepreneurs, Brian Chesky and Joe Gebbia, have just launched a little startup called Airbnb. They're offering air mattresses in their apartment to help pay the rent. It's a novel idea, but bookings are slow, and they're struggling to make ends meet.

Most people in their shoes would've thrown in the towel, chalking it up to a failed experiment. But not Brian and Joe. They knew they were onto something, but they needed to figure out why their offer wasn't quite hitting the mark.

So, they did something brilliant: they started talking to their customers. They reached out to every single person who had booked a stay with them, asking for feedback, suggestions, and insights. They listened carefully, taking meticulous notes and looking for patterns.

And that's when they had their "aha" moment. Their customers loved the idea of staying in a local's home, but they wanted more than just an air mattress on the floor. They wanted a clean, comfortable space with amenities like fresh towels and Wi-Fi.

Armed with this invaluable feedback, Brian and Joe went back to the drawing board. They upgraded their listings. They added more amenities and refined their offer. They did this based on what their customers were telling them. And guess what? Bookings started to soar.

Fast forward a decade, and Airbnb is now a billion-dollar company that has revolutionized the travel industry. But none of that would've been possible if Brian and Joe hadn't taken the time to debrief, analyze their customer feedback, and make pivotal changes to their offer.[18]

And that, my friend, is what this chapter is all about. We're going to dive deep into the art and science of debriefing so you can extract every ounce of insight and value from your validation offer. Just like Brian and Joe, the key to your success lies in listening to your customers and using their feedback to guide your next moves.

So buckle up, grab a notepad, and get ready to learn how to debrief like a pro. Trust me, it's going to be a game-changer for your business.

The Power of Reflection

Let's be real: launching a validation offer is exciting, but it's also exhausting. You've put your heart and soul into making the perfect offer. You've reached out to potential customers and managed all the moving parts. By the time it's all said and done, it's tempting to just move on to the next thing without looking back.

But here's the thing: if you don't take the time to properly debrief and assess your validation offer, you're leaving a goldmine of insights on the table. It's like running a marathon and not bothering to check your time or analyze your performance. Sure, you finished the race, but how do you know if you could've done better?

When you fail to thoroughly debrief, you limit your ability to learn from the experience and make necessary improvements. You might have a vague sense of what worked and what didn't. But, without a process for gathering and analyzing feedback, you're essentially flying blind.

Think about it this way: your validation offer is like a science experiment. You've got a hypothesis (your offer), and you're testing it out in the real world. But, like a scientist, you can't skip the debrief. They wouldn't conduct an experiment without documenting their methods and results.

So, what's the solution? It's simple: you need to follow a clear debriefing process. This process will maximize insights and help you make data-driven decisions about your offer and business model. Ask the right questions. Gather targeted feedback. Analyze your results fairly. This will unlock much knowledge. It will guide your next steps.

Imagine being able to pinpoint why some customers bought your offer while others didn't. Or finding a key feature that could make your offer great. That's the power of a thorough debrief. This is not just about patting yourself on the back for successes. It's about diving into the details. You should use that information to keep improving your offer.

So, if you're serious about turning your validation offer into a success, don't make the mistake of skipping the debrief. Embrace the power of reflection. Follow a clear process. Watch as your insights guide you to a winning offer and a thriving business.

The Three Pillars of Post-Launch Analysis: Feedback, Debrief, and Decision-Making

Congratulations! You've taken the leap and launched your validation offer. You've put your idea out there into the world and now it's time to sit back and relax, right? Not quite.

In fact, this is where the real work begins. It's time to roll up your sleeves and dive into the crucial process of post-launch analysis. This is where you'll gather the insights and data that will guide your next steps and ultimately determine the success of your offer.

So, what does this process look like? It all boils down to three key principles: feedback, debriefing, and decision-making.

Step 1. Gather Feedback

First, let's talk about feedback. After your launch, it's essential to reach out to both your buyers and non-buyers to gather their thoughts and opinions. Why? Because this is your chance to get an inside look at what's working and what's not. Your buyers can tell you what they loved about your offer, what convinced them to make a purchase, and what they think could be improved. Your non-buyers, however, can give valuable insights. They can say what held them back, what didn't resonate, and what might have changed their mind.

Step 2. Do a Proper Debrief

But gathering feedback is just the first step. Next, it's time for the debrief. This is where you'll take a step back and objectively assess your validation offer's performance. It's about looking at the data, analyzing the feedback, and identifying patterns and trends. A proper debrief isn't just a quick glance at your sales numbers; it's a deep dive into the nitty-gritty details of your launch. It's about asking tough questions, confronting what didn't work, and celebrating what did.

Step 3. Decide Your Next Best Move

And finally, armed with the insights from your feedback and debrief, it's time to make your next move. This is where you'll take all that data and transform it into action. You might refine your offer based on customer suggestions. Or pivot to a new approach based on non-buyer objections. Or scale up based on strong positive feedback. The key is to let your insights guide your decision-making process and trust in the power of data-driven action.

Now, I know what you might be thinking: "This all sounds great, but how do I actually do it?" Don't worry, in the coming chapters, we'll dive into the specifics of each of these steps. We'll show you how to gather feedback. Then, how to conduct a thorough debrief. Finally, how to make decisions based on your findings.

But for now, I want you to embrace the power of reflection. Understand that the work doesn't end with your launch; in fact, that's just the beginning. By committing to feedback, debriefing, and decision-making, you're setting yourself up for long-term success. You're not just launching an offer; you're building a foundation for a thriving, customer-centric business.

So, get ready to dive in, get curious, and, most importantly, take action based on your insights. Your validation offer's success story starts now.

Today's Exercise: Reflection on Past Experiences

Before we dive into the nitty-gritty of gathering feedback, debriefing, and making data-driven decisions, let's take a moment to reflect on our own experiences. This exercise will help you understand the value of a thorough post-launch analysis and set the stage for the strategies you'll learn in the coming chapters.

Step 1. Think back to a project, offer, or initiative you launched in the past, whether in your personal or professional life.

Step 2. Write down a brief description of the project, including its goals and outcomes.

Step 3. Reflect on the following questions:

- Did you actively seek feedback from your target audience or customers after the launch? If not, why?

- Did you set aside time for a structured debrief to analyze the project's performance? If yes, what insights did you gain? If not, what held you back?

- Looking back, what decisions did you make based on the project's outcome? Were these decisions data-driven or based on intuition?

Step 4. Now, consider how a more thorough post-launch analysis process, including feedback, debriefing, and data-driven decision-making, could have improved the project's outcome or your next steps.

Step 5. Write down at least one key takeaway or lesson learned from this reflection exercise that you can apply to your current or future projects.

By completing this exercise, you'll start to recognize patterns in your own experiences and understand how a structured post-launch analysis process can lead to better outcomes and more informed decision-making. This is the first step in embracing the power of reflection and setting yourself up for success in your future projects.

In the coming chapters, we'll build on this foundation and explore each step of the post-launch analysis process in detail. You'll learn practical strategies for gathering valuable feedback, conducting a thorough debrief, and making data-driven decisions that will take your projects and offers to the next level.

So, take a moment to complete this reflection exercise, and get ready to dive into the world of post-launch analysis. Your future success stories start here.

Key Takeaways:

- You need a structured debriefing process. It is key for getting the most value and learning from your validation offer.

- The Business Validation Decision Tree and the four magic debrief questions provide powerful frameworks for gathering and analyzing customer feedback.

- Your debrief findings will guide your next moves. They will help you make informed decisions. You can use them to refine, pivot, scale, or leverage your offer for ongoing success.

18

The Business Validation Decision Tree

E ver heard the story of how Dropbox got started? Back in 2007, MIT student Drew Houston was fed up with constantly losing his USB drive. So he started coding a solution: a file storage system that would sync his files across all his computers. Houston knew he was onto something, but when he tried to get investors on board, no one was biting.

You see, online storage wasn't a new idea. Big players like Google and Microsoft were already in the game. So why would anyone want Houston's product? Determined to prove the naysayers wrong, he decided to put out a minimum viable product - a simple video demonstrating how Dropbox worked.

And that's when things got interesting.

Overnight, the video went viral. Houston's beta waiting list skyrocketed from 5,000 to 75,000 people. All because he took a chance and put something out there to validate his idea. He learned that people really did want a simpler way to store and sync their files. Armed with that knowledge, he was able to refine Dropbox into the service millions rely on today.[19]

Houston's story is a perfect example of what this chapter is all about: validating your business idea. See, most people make one of two mistakes. They either barrel ahead with an idea without ever testing the market. Or they put out an initial offer but fail to really evaluate the results and iterate.

Both roads lead to the same destination: a whole lot of wasted time and money.

So what's the solution? It's simple. You need a system to validate your ideas and offers. A way to test the market before going all in. And that's exactly what the Business Idea Decision Tree is all about.

Think of it like a choose-your-own-adventure book for your business. At each step, you'll evaluate a key piece of the puzzle - your audience, your problem, your offer. And based on the results, you'll know exactly what to do next.

Launch a small beta group to gauge interest. Run a free challenge to validate the problem you're solving. Put out a paid workshop to test your offer. And at every turn, you'll be gathering valuable feedback and insights.

So you can ditch the guesswork and make confident, data-driven decisions about where to take your business next. No more throwing spaghetti at the wall and hoping something sticks. With the Business Idea Decision Tree, you'll have a clear roadmap for turning your ideas into viable, profitable offerings.

Ready to dive in? Let's get started.

The Two Traps of Idea Validation

Let's be real. When it comes to validating a business idea, most people fall into one of two traps.

First, there's the "ready, fire, aim" approach. You know the type. They get struck with a lightning bolt of inspiration and charge full steam ahead without ever stopping to test the waters. They pour their heart and soul (and maybe their life savings) into an idea, only to watch it fizzle out faster than a firework in a rainstorm.

Then there's the flip side. The people who dip their toe in the validation pool, but never fully take the plunge. They put out a half-hearted offer, get a lukewarm response, and promptly throw in the towel. "Guess that idea was a dud," they shrug, moving on to the next shiny object.

Both of these approaches rarely work. You might get lucky and hit the jackpot, but chances are, you'll end up watching your chips disappear faster than free donuts in a breakroom.

The truth is that not properly validating your ideas is like setting out on a cross-country road trip without a map. You might have a vague idea of where you want to end up, but without a clear route, you're bound to take a lot of costly detours and dead ends. You'll waste time and resources. You'll chase the wrong audience, solve the wrong problems, or offer the wrong solutions.

And here's the kicker. Even if you do put out an initial offer, failing to carefully evaluate the results is just as dangerous. It's like planting a seed and then abandoning it after a day because it hasn't bloomed yet. Ideas take time and nurturing to grow. If you don't take the time to understand why an offer fell flat, you might be missing out on a golden opportunity to refine and improve.

So, what's the secret to successful idea validation? It's all about mindset.

Treat your initial offers as experiments, not life-or-death trials. Think of it like you're a mad scientist, concocting different formulas in your lab. Some might blow up in your face (metaphorically, we hope), while others could lead to a game-changing discovery.

The key is to launch, then learn. Put something out there, gather feedback, and use it to inform your next move. It's not about perfection, it's about progress.

And that's where the Business Idea Decision Tree comes in. It's like a trusty roadmap for navigating the validation process. At each fork in the road, you'll evaluate a key element of your business - your audience, your problem, your offer. Based on the results, the tree will guide you to your next steps.

Think of it like playing a game of "hot or cold." With each move, you're getting warmer, zeroing in on that sweet spot of product-market fit. And the beauty of the decision tree is that it takes the guesswork out of the equation. No more relying on gut feelings or hunches. Just clear, data-driven actions to keep you on track.

So if you're ready to stop spinning your wheels and start making real progress, it's time to embrace the Business Idea Decision Tree. Get ready to experiment, iterate, and unlock the full potential of your ideas. Your breakthrough is just around the corner.

The Three Steps to Validating Your Business Idea

Ready to put your business idea to the test? It's time to break out the Business Idea Decision Tree. Think of it as your trusty compass for navigating the uncharted waters of idea validation.

Right Audience?

YES   NO

Right Problem?   SURVEY
                                         Float Idea

YES   NO   SURVEY
                             Biggest
                             Challenges

Right Offer?

                 NO   SURVEY
                             Offer
                             Feedback

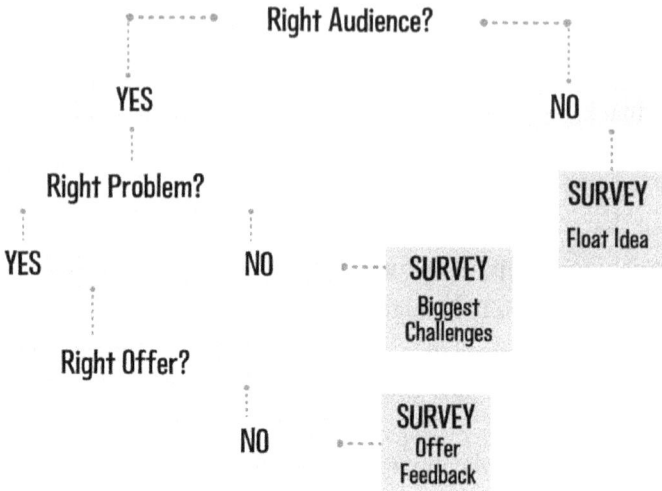

Step 1: Find Your Tribe

First up, we need to make sure you're barking up the right tree when it comes to your audience. After all, even the most brilliant idea will fall flat if you're pitching it to the wrong crowd.

So, how do you find your tribe? It's all about starting small and testing the waters. Whip up a bite-sized offer - maybe a mini course, a virtual workshop, or a 4-week group coaching program. Nothing too fancy or time-consuming, just enough to get a feel for whether your idea resonates.

Then, put it out there and see who bites. Share it with your network, post about it on social media, and shout it from the rooftops (okay, maybe not that last one). The goal is to gauge interest and engagement.

Think of it like trying to complete a puzzle. You might have to try out a few different pieces before you find the ones that fit just right. And that's okay! The key is to stay flexible and keep iterating until you find that perfect match.

Remember, this is just the first step. If you don't hit the bullseye right away, don't throw in the towel. Keep tweaking your idea or your audience until you start to gain some traction.

Step 2: Pinpoint the Pain

Alright, so you've found your people. They're engaged, they're interested, they're ready to rock. Now it's time to dig a little deeper and make sure you're solving the right problem.

Here's the deal. Your audience could be very engaged. But, if you're not addressing a real, pressing pain, your offer will flop.

So how do you validate the problem? Easy. Run a free challenge related to the issue you're trying to solve. Invite your audience to join in and see how they respond.

Are they eager to participate? Are they asking questions, sharing their struggles, and really digging in? Then congratulations, you're on the right track!

But if you're hearing crickets, it might be time to go back to the drawing board. And that's where a little research comes in handy.

Fun fact: According to CB Insights, the number one reason startups fail is because there's no market need. In other words, they're trying to solve a problem that people don't really care about.

So if your challenge isn't gaining traction, don't be afraid to ask your audience what's really keeping them up at night. Send out a survey, hop on some calls, and do a little digging. The answers might surprise you!

And remember, this is all valuable intel. Even if you have to pivot, you're one step closer to cracking the code on a problem that really matters to your people.

Step 3: Get the Scoop

Okay, so you've found your audience and zeroed in on a juicy problem. You're feeling pretty good about this whole validation thing. But before you break out the bubbly, there's one more step.

It's time to gather some feedback.

Maybe you're not quite sure if you're targeting the right folks. Or you've nailed the audience, but you're still not 100% clear on the problem. Or maybe, just maybe, you've got the audience and the problem on lock, but your offer isn't quite hitting the mark.

Never fear; the survey is here!

Seriously though, this is where the magic happens. It's time to go straight to the source and ask your people what they really think.

Not sure about your audience? Float a new idea out there and see how it lands. Struggling to pinpoint the right problem? Ask your email list or social media followers about their biggest challenges. Offer falling flat? Reach out to those who didn't buy and find out why.

The key is to gather as much data as you can. Once you have that precious feedback in hand, you'll be ready to take your offer to the next level.

Just look at Uber. When they first launched, their initial offer was a total flop. But did they give up? No way. They listened to their users, made some tweaks, and kept on iterating. And now, well, you know the rest.

So don't be afraid to ask for feedback, even if it stings a little. Every piece of input is a clue, a breadcrumb leading you closer to that pot of gold at the end of the validation rainbow.

And once you've got all that juicy data? Well, that's where the real fun begins. But we'll save that for the next chapter.

For now, just remember: validate, iterate, and always, always keep your ear to the ground. Your audience holds the key to unlocking your idea's full potential. All you have to do is listen.

Today's Exercise: Implement the Business Validation Decision Tree

Alright, it's time to get our hands dirty and put the Business Idea Decision Tree to work. This is where the rubber meets the road, folks. Where we separate the validation pros from the wantrepreneurs.

So block off the next 10-15 minutes, silence your phone, and put on your thinking cap. It's time to give your validation offer a good, hard look.

First, pull up the Business Idea Decision Tree. Now, take a stroll through each step and evaluate how your offer stacks up.

- **Question 1.** Were you able to generate excitement about your topic idea? If the answer is yes, go to question two. If no, then give it a few weeks and try a new topic or different audience (after you survey your list and social for more topic ideas).

- **Question 2.** Did you tackle a problem people were willing to pay for? If the answer is yes, go to question three. If no, ask people what their biggest challenges are when it comes to the topic.

- **Question 3.** Did you get a decent amount of sales? If yes, congrats! If no, send an email to all the non-buyers. Ask them to reply to your email and share with them why they decided not to buy at this time. Collect what they mention to you.

Did you find your tribe, or are you still searching for that perfect audience match? Did your free challenge strike a chord, or did it fall on deaf ears? Are people whipping out their wallets for your paid offer, or is your checkout page gathering virtual cobwebs?

Be honest with yourself. This isn't the time for rose-colored glasses or wishful thinking. The more brutally honest you are, the better equipped you'll be to make smart, strategic moves.

Now, here's where it gets juicy. Look at where you're getting stuck on the tree. Is it the audience branch? The problem branch? The offer branch? Wherever you're hitting a snag, that's where you'll want to focus your energy.

It's time to get creative. Brainstorm at least three experiments you could run to unstick yourself and level up your validation game. And don't be afraid to think outside the box!

Maybe you need to test out a new audience by partnering with an influencer in a different niche. Or perhaps you could run a series of polls to uncover the problems that really keep your people up at night. Or what if you tweaked your offer to include a juicy bonus or a payment plan?

So take a deep breath, roll up your sleeves, and get ready to experiment like a mad scientist. The Business Idea Decision Tree is your trusty sidekick, and those three experiments are your secret weapons.

Now go forth and validate like a boss. Your breakthrough is waiting.

Key Takeaways:

- Validation isn't a one-time event but an ongoing process. Keep iterating based on feedback until you reach product-market fit.

- Use the Business Validation Decision Tree framework. Use it to methodically diagnose issues with the audience, problem, or offer. Then, use it to determine the right adjustments to make.

- You launch, and then you learn. The key to successful validation is maintaining an experimenter's mindset. Treat everything as a learning opportunity to refine and improve.

19

The Magic of the Debrief

I n the heat of the Vietnam War, the U.S. Army found itself in a quandary. They had more and better weapons. But, they struggled to gain an advantage. This was due to the Viet Cong's unusual guerrilla tactics. Frustration and demoralization set in as the Army grappled with how to adapt and overcome.

Enter the After Action Review (AAR). The Army developed the AAR during this hard period. It was a groundbreaking process. It helped soldiers learn from their experiences and get better. The concept was simple but powerful. After each mission, soldiers would meet to discuss three key questions: What happened? What went well? What could be improved for future missions?

By examining their successes and failures, soldiers could find areas for improvement. They could then make needed changes to their strategies and tactics. The AAR fostered a culture of learning, adaptability, and growth in the Army. This culture led to better performance and outcomes in battle.

The impact of the AAR was so profound that it quickly spread throughout the U.S. military and beyond. Today, the AAR is a standard practice in militaries worldwide. Its ideas have been adopted by businesses and groups in many industries.[20]

So, what does this mean for you and your launches? The answer is simple: debriefing is your secret weapon.

Like the Army's AAR, a good debrief after each launch can give you valuable insights. It will set you up for future success. Take time to think about what worked, what didn't, and what can be improved. Then, you'll be able to make data-driven decisions and optimizations that will greatly improve your next launch.

In the next sections, we'll explore the steps and strategies you need to use. They will make debriefing a key part of your launch process. We'll cover how to structure your debriefs. We'll talk about what questions to ask. And, how to turn your findings into actionable improvements.

Because here's the truth: launching is just the beginning. The real magic happens in the debrief. It's where you'll uncover the insights and opportunities that will take your launches from good to great.

So, get ready to embrace the power of the debrief. Your future launches (and your bottom line) will thank you.

Debrief or Bust: The Costly Mistake of Rushing to the Next Thing

You've just wrapped up a big launch. You poured your heart and soul into it, burning the midnight oil and hustling like there's no tomorrow. The moment it's over, you breathe a sigh of relief and immediately start thinking about what's next on your to-do list. Sound familiar?

If you're like most entrepreneurs, you probably have a tendency to jump straight from one launch to the next without taking a beat. You're eager to keep the momentum going, to capitalize on the buzz, to strike while the iron's hot. But here's the thing: when you skip the debrief, you're doing yourself a huge disservice.

Sure, it might feel productive to dive headfirst into your next project, but you're missing out on a golden opportunity to learn, grow, and optimize. By not taking the time to reflect on what worked, what didn't, and what could be improved, you're essentially flying blind. You're making decisions based on gut instinct rather than data-driven insights.

And that's a recipe for stagnation.

When you don't debrief, you risk repeating the same mistakes over and over again. You fail to capitalize on your successes and miss out on chances to double down on what's working. You rob yourself of the opportunity to iterate, innovate, and take your launches to the next level.

But here's the good news: there's a simple solution. Implement a structured debrief process. It will capture all those juicy learnings and insights. Then, use them to inform your future launches.

A solid debrief is like a treasure map, guiding you toward the gold mines of optimization and success. It's a chance to step back, assess your performance, and identify areas for improvement. It's an opportunity to celebrate your wins, learn from your losses, and chart a course for even greater success.

So, how do you make debriefing a non-negotiable part of your launch process? It all starts with a commitment to reflection and a willingness to confront the good, the bad, and the ugly. In the next section, we'll dive into the nitty-gritty of how to structure your debriefs for maximum impact.

But first, let's make a pact: no more launch-and-leave. No more rushing to the next thing without pausing to reflect. No more missed opportunities for growth and optimization.

The Magic of the Debrief: 5 Steps to Uncovering Your Next Goldmine Idea

Step 1: Create a Dedicated Debrief Spreadsheet

Your debrief spreadsheet is your launch's best friend. This hub captures all your thoughts, ideas, and customer feedback. It also collects feedback from non-customers. Think of it as the ultimate brain dump for your launch.

Just like how athletes obsessively review game footage to identify areas for improvement, your debrief spreadsheet allows you to analyze your launch from every possible angle. It's your chance to get granular, to dig deep, and to uncover those game-changing insights.

So, what goes into this magical spreadsheet? Everything. Every bit of feedback, every idea that pops into your head, every data point you can get your hands on. The more comprehensive your spreadsheet, the more powerful your debrief will be.

Remember: a well-organized debrief spreadsheet is the foundation for a successful debrief process. It's the bedrock upon which you'll build your future launch strategies. So, take the time to set it up right, and watch as it becomes your secret weapon for optimization and growth.

Step 2: Identify What to "Do Again"

You nailed it. Those elements of your launch that worked like a charm, that had your customers raving and your metrics soaring? Those are the things you want to bottle up and replicate in every future launch.

In this step, your mission is to pinpoint those success factors and make them your north star. Dig through your feedback, your data, and your own observations to identify what really moved the needle. Was it a particular marketing strategy? A killer piece of content? A influencer partnership that set your launch on fire?

Whatever it was, make a note of it in your spreadsheet. These are the things you want to double down on to make a core part of your launch playbook.

As Winston Churchill famously said, "Success is not final, failure is not fatal: it is the courage to continue that counts." Recognizing and leveraging your successes is key to building momentum and consistency. So, don't be shy about patting yourself on the back and making those wins a central part of your go-forward strategy.

Step 3: Determine What to "Do Differently"

Hindsight is 20/20, right? Looking back on your launch, there are probably a few things that you'd approach differently if you had a do-over. Maybe that Facebook ad campaign fell flat, or that webinar didn't quite hit the mark.

In this step, your job is to reflect on those aspects of your launch that didn't quite live up to your expectations. This isn't about beating yourself up – it's about learning and growing.

As Thomas Edison famously said, "I have not failed. I've just found 10,000 ways that won't work." Embracing and learning from your missteps is essential for growth and improvement.

So, take a hard look at what didn't work, and brainstorm ways to approach things differently next time. Would a different ad platform have yielded better results? Could you have tweaked your webinar content to be more engaging?

Capture those insights in your spreadsheet and use them to inform your future launch strategies. Remember: every "failure" is just a stepping stone on the path to success.

Step 4: Identify What to "Start Doing"

Innovation is the name of the game. You need to stay ahead of the curve. You need to keep your launches fresh and effective. So, you need to always look for new strategies, tactics, and ideas.

In this step, your job is to brainstorm new approaches. You didn't use them in your last launch, but they could make your future launches better.

Maybe you've been hearing buzz about a new social media platform that your target audience is flocking to. Or perhaps there's a new content format that's been generating tons of engagement in your industry.

The possibilities are endless – the key is to keep an open mind and be willing to experiment. So, don't be afraid to think outside the box and try something new. Capture those ideas in your spreadsheet, and make a plan to test them out in your next launch.

Remember: continuously seeking out new opportunities and ideas is crucial for staying ahead of the curve. Embrace the unknown, and watch your launches soar.

Step 5: Decide What to "Stop Doing"

Sometimes, less is more. Just as a gardener prunes dead branches to promote growth, cutting ineffective practices lets you focus on what truly matters.

In this final step, your job is to take a hard look at your launch and identify the activities or efforts that yielded little to no results. Perhaps you poured hours into crafting the perfect email sequence, only to see abysmal open rates. Or maybe you invested in a pricey tool that ended up being more trouble than it was worth.

Whatever the case may be, it's time to cut the dead weight. Streamlining your efforts by eliminating what doesn't work is just as important as identifying what does.

So, comb through your spreadsheet and ruthlessly identify those areas where you didn't see a solid return on your investment. Make a note to either tweak your approach or ditch those practices altogether in your next launch.

Remember: your time and resources are precious. By cutting out the ineffective stuff, you free yourself up to double down on the strategies and tactics that really move the needle.

And there you have it – the five steps to a killer debrief spreadsheet and process. By following this approach after every launch, you'll be able to keep improving. You'll make your strategies better and your results too. You'll take your business to new heights.

Today's Exercise: Complete Your Debrief

Alright, it's time to put all this debrief knowledge into practice. Grab a timer, set it for 15 minutes, and let's dive into a real-life debrief of your most recent launch.

First things first: crack open a fresh spreadsheet. You know the drill by now – this is where you'll capture all those juicy insights and aha moments.

Now, cast your mind back to your last launch. Take a deep breath, and let's break it down using the four categories we've been talking about.

Category #1: Do Again. What worked like a charm? What had your customers raving and your metrics soaring? Jot down those success factors in your spreadsheet. These are the things you want to make a staple in your launch playbook.

Category #2: Do Differently. Hindsight is a beautiful thing. Looking back, what would you change? What didn't quite hit the mark? Put those insights in your spreadsheet. Then, brainstorm ways to do things differently next time.

Category #3: Start Doing. It's time to get innovative. What new strategies, tactics, or ideas could you experiment with in your next launch? Let your imagination run wild, and capture those lightbulb moments in your spreadsheet.

Category #4: Stop Doing. Trim the fat. What activities or efforts didn't yield results? What felt like a waste of time or resources? Make a note in your spreadsheet to ditch those practices in your next launch.

Set that timer and go! Spend 15 focused minutes really digging into your last launch. Be honest with yourself, and don't hold back. The more comprehensive your debrief, the more powerful your insights will be.

Once your timer dings, take a step back and review your notes. What patterns do you see? What insights jump out at you? Use those observations to craft a killer action plan for your next launch.

Maybe you realized that your social media strategy needs a serious overhaul. Perhaps you identified a new content format that you want to experiment with. Whatever the case may be, translate those insights into concrete action steps.

Remember: your debrief is only as valuable as what you do with it. So, don't let those insights gather dust in your spreadsheet. Put them into action, and watch as your launches get better and better with each iteration.

Congratulations – you just completed your first real-life launch debrief! How do you feel? Energized? Inspired? Ready to tackle your next launch with newfound clarity and purpose?

That's the power of the debrief, my friend. Make this a regular practice after every launch. Then, you'll be able to continuously improve your strategies and results. This will take your business to new heights.

So, keep that debrief spreadsheet close, and make reflection a non-negotiable part of your launch process. Your future self (and your bottom line) will thank you.

Key Takeaways:

- Thorough debriefs after each launch are essential. They allow for continuous improvement and future success.

- A structured debrief process uses the four categories. They are: Do Again, Do Differently, Start Doing, and Stop Doing. This process helps find key insights and growth opportunities.

- Debrief insights lead to successful launches and industry innovation. They provide a competitive edge by driving increases in both areas.

20
Deciding Your Next Move

T homas Edison hunched over his workbench, surrounded by a graveyard of failed experiments. Filaments, glass bulbs, wires - all testaments to his relentless pursuit of a world-changing idea. The electric light bulb.

But here's the thing. Edison didn't just wake up one morning, screw in a bulb, and voila, let there be light! No, his journey was a series of validation offers. Each failed attempt was a tiny workshop, a mini-course on what doesn't work.

You see, Edison understood something most folks miss. Failure isn't the end of the road. It's just a signpost pointing you in a new direction. Every busted bulb was a debrief, a chance to survey the results and decide his next move.[21]

And that's precisely what we're diving into in this chapter. You've put your idea out there, tested the waters with your validation offer. Now it's time to parse that feedback and chart your course forward.

Will you stick with the same topic but level up your offer? Maybe you'll keep the format but switch gears to a new subject. Or perhaps you'll double down on a winning idea and build it out into something bigger.

The beauty is there's no one "right" path. But, by following in Edison's footsteps and treating each effort as a chance to learn, you'll light the way to a brighter future for your business.

So grab your metaphorical toolbox, and let's get ready to tinker, tweak, and transform your validation offer into a beacon of success. If Edison can light up the world one experiment at a time, just imagine what you can achieve by deciding your next move with intention and insight.

How to Decide Your Next Move

You've poured your heart into your validation offer, launched it out into the world, and now you're staring at the feedback rolling in. Cue the drumroll, right? But wait, what's this? Crickets, confusion, maybe even a sprinkle of criticism. Ouch.

Here's where most prople stumble. They either slam on the blinders and barrel ahead with their original plan, ignoring the writing on the wall. Or they throw up their hands in defeat, convinced their idea is a dud.

But here's the thing: both of those knee-jerk reactions are a fast track to nowhere. When you tune out feedback, you're missing out on a goldmine of intel that could help you polish your offer to a high shine.

So, what's the move? Embrace the feedback, warts and all. Treat it like a trusted advisor, whispering secrets to success in your ear. Your validation offer isn't the final destination; it's just the first pit stop on a winding road.

Think of it like dating. You wouldn't expect to meet your soulmate on the first blind date, right? No, you'd gather info, adjust your approach, and maybe even tweak your profile pic. Building a business is no different. Each validation offer is a chance to learn, adapt, and come back stronger.

So take a deep breath, put on your detective hat, and get ready to mine that feedback for all it's worth. When you view your validation offer as one chapter in a longer story, you'll be amazed at the plot twists and triumphs waiting just around the bend.

Alright, let's dive in. You've got your feedback, you've sifted through the insights. Now it's time to decide your next move. But here's the beautiful thing: there's no singular "right" path. You've got options, and we're about to explore four potential game plans.

Four Paths to Consider

You've taken a brave step and put your ideas to the test. Whether the response was overwhelming or underwhelming, you've gained invaluable insights. Now, it's time to decide your next move.

Outcome 1. Same Offer Type, Same Topic

If your offer showed promise, consider running it again. You've likely just scratched the surface of your potential audience. Many who missed out initially will appreciate a second chance to get in on the action.

Learn from Broadway hits: Hamilton and others do trial runs in smaller cities. They make tweaks based on feedback. Then, they take the refined version to the big stage. You can follow the same script: make strategic improvements to your initial offer and relaunch it with confidence.

Maybe you increase the price to reflect the value you're providing. Maybe you revamp the sales page to better speak to your ideal client's desires. Maybe you can add a powerful new strategy that didn't occur to you the first time around.

The key takeaway? When you've got a winner, double down. Let your initial success fuel even greater success.

Outcome 2. Same Offer Type, Different Topic

Perhaps it's not the offer itself that needs a remix - it's the subject matter. If you found yourself energized by the process of leading a one-day workshop or a month-long bootcamp, stick with that winning format. Just swap in a new theme that better resonates with your target audience.

Think of it as a master chef keeping their signature style but changing up the ingredients based on what's fresh and in-season. Give your audience the specific transformation they're craving in the container that lights you up. It's a recipe for success!

Outcome 3. Same Offer Type, Same Topic (But Expand to Main Offer)

If your validation offer struck a chord content-wise, it may be time to expand your scope. You've given your audience a taste of what you have to offer - now, invite them to pull up a chair and feast!

Consider splitting your short workshop into a detailed course. Turn your one-on-one coaching session into a life-changing group program. You've seen the demand for your core topic; don't be afraid to go all in and create the definitive resource on the subject.

Outcome 4. Different Validation Offer, New Topic

Maybe you're itching to shake things up completely. A new format, a wildly different topic - something that feels equal parts thrilling and terrifying. Guess what? That's what validation offers are for! You have full permission to test the waters with an unconventional idea.

Think of it like being an angel investor. You're not risking your entire livelihood on a single, untested concept. You're making small, strategic bets to see what gains traction. Some may fizzle out, while others might just become the next big thing. The key is to experiment often and pivot quickly.

Bonus Move: Map Out a One-Year Profit Calendar

To really capitalize on the power of validation offers, try mapping out an entire year's worth. Imagine holding a crystal ball, but instead of a hazy future, you see a clear roadmap to consistent revenue.

You might schedule a quarterly workshop. It feeds into a key course, which leads to an application-only mastermind. Or perhaps you host a monthly bootcamp, each focused on a different hot topic in your niche. The exact composition will depend on your business and your audience, but the principle is the same:

Treat validation offers not as a one-off experiment but as the building blocks of a sustainable, scalable business. With each offer, you're not just testing an idea - you're adding a new income stream and strengthening your foundation.

Remember, as the legendary Peter Drucker said, "The best way to predict the future is to create it." So go forth and validate with gusto! Your ideal audience is waiting for you to lead the way.

Today's Exercise: Brainstorming Your Next Move

You've gained valuable insights from your initial validation offer. Now, it's time to harness that momentum and plan your next steps. One powerful way to do this is through a focused brainstorming session.

Set aside just 15 minutes – you'll be amazed at what you can come up with in this short burst of concentrated creativity. Grab a pen and paper, or open up a fresh document on your computer. Then, set a timer and let the ideas flow.

During this brainstorming sprint, consider the four potential paths forward:

1. **Sticking with what's working:** Could you run the same offer on the same topic again, perhaps with some minor improvements based on feedback?

2. **Keeping the format, changing the topic:** Did you love the process of leading a particular type of offer (like a one-day workshop or a multi-week bootcamp)? Could you apply that same format to a different subject that might resonate even more with your audience?

3. **Going deeper on a winning topic:** If your validation offer struck a chord content-wise, how could you expand on that theme? Could you turn a short workshop into a comprehensive course or a one-time coaching session into an ongoing group program?

4. **Experimenting with a whole new concept:** Is there a completely different offer format or topic that you're itching to test out? Something that feels equal parts exciting and

scary? Jot down those wild ideas – they just might be your next big breakthrough.

As you brainstorm, don't worry about perfecting each idea or deciding which ones are "good enough." The goal of this exercise is simply to generate possibilities – you'll have plenty of time to refine and evaluate them later.

If you find yourself getting stuck, try asking yourself some prompting questions:

- What topics do my clients or customers bring up most often?

- What skills or knowledge do I have that I haven't fully shared yet?

- What emerging trends or technologies could I tap into?

- What's a contrarian view in my industry that I could explore?

- How could I put a fresh spin on a classic topic or format?

Remember, this brainstorming session is a judgment-free zone. No idea is too big, too small, or too "out there." You never know which seemingly random thought might spark your next great offering.

Once the timer goes off, take a quick break to rest your mental muscles. Then, come back to your list with fresh eyes. Look for any themes or patterns that emerge. Circle or highlight the ideas that feel most energizing or promising.

You might not settle on a single, clear direction right away – and that's okay. Let the ideas marinate a bit. Sleep on them, talk them over with a trusted colleague or mentor, do some further research. The right path forward will become clear in time.

The key is to keep the momentum going. Don't let the insights from your initial validation offer go to waste. Use this brainstorming exercise as a launching pad for your next steps.

You can repeat a winning formula. You can remix a proven format. You can dive deeper into a resonant topic. Or, you can brave uncharted territory. Trust that you're on the right track. Each validation offer is a stepping stone to a more impactful, more profitable business. You've got this!

Key Takeaways:

- Audience feedback is a goldmine of insights to refine your offer. Use it to make informed decisions, not as a final verdict.

- After a validation offer, you can repeat what worked, keep the format but change the topic, expand a winning topic, or test something new. Let feedback guide you.

- Plan a 1-year sequence of validation offers for an action plan to grow your business iteratively. Adjust based on market response.

21

The Validate Your Offer 28-Day Action Plan

C ongratulations on completing this journey to validating your offer! You should feel proud of taking this important first step to turning your ideas into income.

It's normal to feel a little uncertain as you put your offer out there. Just remember - your solution matters. Your unique approach can help and inspire others facing similar challenges. We all start unsure of ourselves. But your authentic offer carries power no generic product alone ever could.

Focus on serving whoever needs your offer most. Create from the heart, no matter the size of your audience today. Some of history's most influential products started small before catching fire based on the value they gave.

You now have all the tools needed to overcome common hurdles standing between new creators like yourself and success. This book equips you to handle offer creation, validation, optimization, and everything in between. So whenever self-doubt creeps in, recall the guidance these pages contain.

Your dream to impact lives through your writing, coaching, teaching, or speaking is absolutely within reach. Our world needs more problem-solvers and innovators - exactly what you offer. Feel optimistic knowing everything that brought you here has prepared you for what comes next. I applaud you for undertaking this fulfilling yet challenging path. Now go make your unique mark!

If you prefer going through this material with a physical workbook, be sure to check out the Validate Your Offer Companion Workbook. This supplementary guide contains all the exercises from the book in a convenient print format. Completing them with paper and pen can help the lessons stick even more.

Refer back any time you need motivation or want to revisit the core principles that empowered your offer validation. Having an offline reference helps many people process, retain, and apply these essential concepts.

You can learn more at PlatformGrowthBooks.com.

So, pick up the workbook if you learn best by writing rather than reading digitally. Either way, you now hold the keys to success!

The Validate Your Offer 28-Day Action Plan

Day 1: Choose your validation offer type (low-content book, mini-course, 4-week bootcamp, or virtual workshop)

Day 2: Select your validation offer topic

Day 3: Set your validation offer timeline (14, 21, or 28 days)

Day 4: Define your offer's key outcome or transformation

Day 5: Identify your audience's main problems related to your offer

Day 6: Craft a clear, compelling promise for your offer

Day 7: Outline the 3-5 key steps to achieve the desired outcome

Day 8: Create a master layout for your core content pages (for low-content books)

Day 9: Develop your mini-course structure and key lessons (for mini-courses)

Day 10: Plan your 4-week bootcamp curriculum (for group coaching)

Day 11: Design your virtual workshop agenda (for speakers)

Day 12: Write your offer's headline and subheading

Day 13: Use the "Who, What, Why, How" script to structure your sales page content

Day 14: Highlight the key benefits and outcomes of your offer on your sales page

Day 15: Include a clear call-to-action and risk-reversal strategy on your sales page

Day 16: Conduct a Potential Audience Audit to uncover your hidden audience

Day 17: Identify strategies to appeal to the 4 types of buyers (spontaneous, methodical, social proof, and deadline-driven)

Day 18: Build anticipation for your offer launch through sneak peeks and teasers

Day 19: Generate buzz by encouraging social sharing and leveraging influencers

Day 20: Open your offer cart with urgency (limited time or scarcity)

Day 21: Deliver and exceed expectations with your validation offer

Day 22: Consider offer stacking to serve customers at different price points and stages

Day 23: Create a dedicated Debrief Spreadsheet to capture feedback and insights

Day 24: Identify what worked well in your offer to replicate in the future

Day 25: Determine what you would do differently next time based on feedback

Day 26: Brainstorm new strategies and ideas to start implementing in future offers

Day 27: Decide what to stop doing based on low performance or ROI

Day 28: Choose your next move (same offer type/topic, new offer type/topic, or expand to main offer)

Follow this 28-day action plan. It will help you validate your idea. You'll also gather valuable feedback and make data-driven choices for your next steps. Remember, launching is just the beginning – the real magic happens in the debrief and iteration process. Trust the journey and keep experimenting!

Thank You

I want to express my gratitude for choosing and purchasing my book. In a world overflowing with choices, you selected mine, and for that, I'm truly thankful.

Before we part ways, may I request a minor favor? Would it be too much to ask for you to leave a review on the platform? For an independent author like myself, receiving direct reader feedback through reviews significantly contributes to the success of the work.

Your insights will guide me in creating content that effectively aids you in achieving your desired results. Your feedback is highly valuable to me. Thank you for your time and consideration.

Leave a review by going to: **JMill.Biz/Validate-Review**

22
What's Next?

Congratulations on completing your journey through "Validate Your Offer: A 28-Day Profit Plan to Test the Market First and Turn Ideas into Income as a Writer, Coach, Teacher, or Speaker"! By now, you've mastered the art of crafting compelling validation offers that resonate with your target audience and generate real revenue.

But as you celebrate this milestone, you might be wondering, "What's next?" Once you've successfully validated your offer, where should you focus your energy to keep the momentum going and scale your impact?

Whenever my private clients ask this question, my response is always the same: "It's time to build your audience!"

You see, validating your offer is a crucial first step, but to truly grow a thriving business, you need a steady stream of leads and customers. And the key to attracting those eager buyers is by building a loyal, engaged audience around your brand.

But here's the thing: growing an audience can feel overwhelming, especially if you're new to the online space. With so many platforms, strategies, and tactics to choose from, it's easy to get stuck in analysis paralysis and fail to take consistent action.

That's why I've distilled the process down to just four essential traffic methods that any writer, coach, teacher, or speaker can use to grow their audience quickly and efficiently:

- Boost - increasing your social media engagement and leads effortlessly

- Build - creating an automated organic content engine with blogs, podcasts, and YouTube videos

- Borrow - collaborating with other experts to reach new audiences and provide value to their communities.

- Buy - using paid ads effectively and simply to expand your reach

Each of these methods, when implemented strategically, can help you attract a flood of targeted leads and potential customers to your online platform. And the best part? You don't need to be a tech wizard or marketing genius to make them work for your business.

Want to know the step-by-step playbook for implementing these four traffic methods and building an audience of raving fans?

That's exactly what I cover in depth in the fourth book of this series: "Build Your Audience: The 60-Day Traffic Playbook to Instantly Increase Your Leads and Sales as a Writer, Coach, or Speaker."

Inside, you'll discover:

- The secret to boosting your social media engagement and generating leads on autopilot

- How to create a content machine that attracts your ideal clients 24/7

- The art of borrowing other people's audiences to skyrocket your own

- The simple, stress-free approach to using paid ads for rapid growth

- And much more!

If you're ready to take your business to the next level and start attracting a steady stream of eager buyers, then "Build Your Audience" is your essential roadmap.

Don't let your validated offer sit on the virtual shelf, gathering dust. It's time to get it in front of the people who need it most, and watch your impact and income soar.

Grab your copy of "Build Your Audience: The 60-Day Traffic Playbook to Instantly Increase Your Leads and Sales as a Writer, Coach, or Speaker" today at: PlatformGrowthBooks.com

Your audience is waiting for you. Let's go build it together!

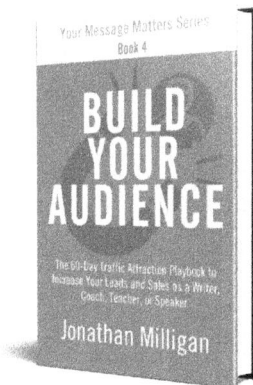

1. "Supermarine Spitfire." *Encyclopaedia Britannica*, 16 May 2024, www.britannica.com/biography/R-J-Mitchell. Accessed 31 May 2024.

2. Godin, Seth. "Build it, and they will come' only works in the movies. Social Media is a 'build it, nurture it, engage them, and they may come and stay.'" *Scattered Quotes*, 31 May 2020, scatteredquotes.com/build-it-and-they-will-come/. Accessed 31 May 2024.

3. Westervelt, Eric. "From YouTube Pioneer Sal Khan, A School with Real Classrooms." NPR, 30 June 2016, www.npr.org/2016/06/30/483163734/from-youtube-pioneer-sal-khan-a-school-with-real-classrooms. Accessed 31 May 2024.

4. "History & Culture - Pony Express National Historic Trail." U.S. National Park Service, www.nps.gov/poex/learn/historyculture/index.htm. Accessed 31 May 2024.

5. Skyway to Wonderland. "Walt & His Inspiration for Disneyland Opening Day Attractions." *Skyway to Wonderland*, www.skywaytowonderland.com/walt-disney-inspiration-disneyland. Accessed 31 May 2024.

6. Parkinson, Cyril Northcote. "Parkinson's Law—Or the Rising Pyramid." *The Economist*, 19 Nov. 1955.

7. Smithy, Lewis J. "The Four Act Structure: What It Is + How It Works." *The Novel Smithy*, 18 May 2021, www.thenovelsmithy.com/four-act-structure. Accessed 31 May 2024.

8. "Remembering the First Publication of the Poor Richard's Almanack." *National Council of Teachers of English*, 26 Dec. 2021, https://ncte.org/blog/2021/12/remembering-first-publication-poor-richards-almanack/.

9. "Tin Pan Alley." *Encyclopaedia Britannica*, Encyclopaedia Britannica, www.britannica.com/art/Tin-Pan-Alley-musical-history.

10. Garvens, John. "Earn1k Review: From No Ideas to $150 per Hour on the Side." John Garvens, 18 May 2023, www.johngarvens.com/earn1k-review.

11. "The 1950s Science and Technology: Overview." *Encyclopedia.com*, UXL American Decades, www.encyclopedia.com/social-sciences/culture-magazines/1950s-science-and-technology-overview. Accessed 31 May 2024.

12. Hevesi, Dennis. "Barry Becher, a Creator of Ginsu Knife Commercials, Dies at 71." *The New York Times*, 30 June 2012. Retrieved 1 April 2023.

13. Sax, Boria. "The Great Beanie Baby Marketing Strategy." *Source Marketing Material*, 27 February 2024. www.sourcemarketingmaterial.com/the-great-beanie-baby-marketing-strategy. Accessed 31 May 2024.

14. "J.K. Rowling - Harry Potter Books Author." Bloomsbury, www.bloomsbury.com/jk-rowling. Accessed 31 May 2024.

15. "David Ogilvy: The Father of Advertising." The Drum, www.thedrum.com/david-ogilvy. Accessed 31 May 2024.

16. Milligan, Ceara. "Here's How Much That Popeyes Chicken Sandwich Tweet Was Actually Worth." *Mashed*, 24 April 2022, www.mashed.com/841845/heres-how-much-that-popeyes-chicken-sandwich-tweet-was-actually-worth/. Accessed 31 May 2024.

17. Nathan, James. "Would You Like Fries With That? What McDonalds Can Teach Us about Cross-Selling." *The James Nathan Experience*, 19 Sept. 2017, www.jamesnathan.com/mcdonalds-cross-selling. Accessed 31 May 2024.

18. "Airbnb Startup Story: The Journey of Airbnb Founder Brian Chesky." *Bold Business*, 2021, www.boldbusiness.com/airbnb-startup-story/.

19. "From Startup to $12 Billion: Seven Lessons from Dropbox." *MIT News*, Massachusetts Institute of Technology, 2021, news.mit.edu/2018/dropbox-startup-12-billion-0620.

20. "Emergent Learning in Action: The After Action Review." *The Systems Thinker*, www.thesystemsthinker.com/emergent-learning-in-action-the-after-action-review. Accessed 31 May 2024.

21. Bellis, Mary. "The Failed Inventions of Thomas Alva Edison." *ThoughtCo*, 5 Apr. 2023, www.thoughtco.com/thomas-edison-failures-1991687.